Nicholas Malaos

MODERNITY
How the Medium Became the Message

Copyright © 2018 by Nicholas Malaos

Printed in the United Kingdom

All rights reserved. No part of this book may be reproduced or transmitted in any form or by any means, electronic or mechanical, including photocopying or recording without the permission of the author.

Cover design and layout by www.spiffingcovers.com

About The Author

Nicholas Malaos was born in New York City. He attended Columbia University as an undergraduate, studying philosophy, humanities and contemporary civilisation. A British resident the whole of his adult life, he now divides his time between London and the southern Peloponnese, in Greece.

Introduction

In a humorous and sometimes cynical tone, Nicholas Malaos demonstrates how our concept of the present is underpinned by our vast past, yet we cannot see that which is immediately before us. Absorbed in the patterns of behaviour that constitute our daily existence, we remain oblivious to larger and graver concerns. Slaves to modishness, to transient values and precepts, we are unable to assess, with objectivity, the merits and disadvantages of *the way we live*.

Generational changes in attitudes, popular culture and lifestyle are not difficult to see, but the underlying causes are far less recognisable. Malaos eloquently asserts that our situation is forever 'morphing', being shaped and reshaped, and not merely by the obvious effects of ever-advancing technology. More direct influences are to be found in commercialisation, the associated trends in consumerism, and the natural yet worrying human tendency to be 'conditioned' by what is popular and fashionable.

With insightful forays into history and philosophy, the author suggests that throughout the development of Western thought and culture, a consistent obstacle to progress and enlightenment has been our inability to define objective truth or *dogmatic* certainty. Indeed, the claim is made that insights *of* the moment seldom emerge *from* the moment. It is best left for subsequent generations to look back in judgement, with the detachment and wisdom afforded by the passage of time.

Chapter 1
There was a Time...

People used to wear shoes. Now the footwear of choice consists largely of something best described as 'designer trainers'. Periodically re-heeled and re-soled, shoes lasted for years, sometimes a lifetime. Trainers are disposable, and contrived to be so, deliberately manufactured for a limited lifespan, a newly purchased pair to regale the feet as the old one is discarded. 'Planned obsolescence' is a recent tactic of strategic marketing, the corporate commercial world's device for social and demographic engineering, consumer manipulation and 'trend-setting'. Its application has impelled shoe-repair shops to diversify, turning to such additional services as key-cutting, engraving and watch repairs – just to stay in business. Shoemakers have slowly morphed into jewellers.

There was a time when a young man would be inspired to sing under the balcony of a lady to whom he was attracted. It was a practice known as 'serenading'. Not quite the thing to do any more. In the light of current social convention and all appurtenances of modern middle-class life, 'folksy' or 'laughable' would understate any assessment of such an activity. Yet, as a ritualised expression of personal interest, it was 'the done thing' in much of Mediterranean Europe for centuries, as remarkable as it may strike us today, right up to the 1950's. A reality of its time, serenading was appropriated by nearly every form of popular entertainment, and even in cultures of the world where not traditionally practised, it made its way into public awareness through literary classics. Though later emerging as a feature of blatantly escapist worlds when depicted in low-budget Hollywood musicals of the 1930's, it remained, nonetheless, scarcely a type of protocol confined to 'Ruritania'. It was real, however enduring its portrayal as a caricature of life. That publishers of books of etiquette and modern manners – Debrett and others – take annual updates as seriously as they do, is just as well. Rapid social change is, by all accounts in our post-industrial world, a direct function of ever-accelerating technological advancement.

By today's codes of conduct, any comparable young man, far from entertaining thoughts of crooning under a balcony, would still be subject to the influence of popular culture – inescapably so. For any object of his infatuation, peremptory facial snaps via the internet would be par for the course. But, as an afterthought, he may also be tempted to upload photographs of decidedly more piquant parts of his anatomy; new conventions for a new age. Why the need for a balcony when you have broadband? Besides which, northern climes are not conducive to spending time in outdoor spaces, or to gaining such easy access to them as may be had from salons or boudoirs. In this 'sceptred isle', architectural purposes of 'function', as opposed to 'form', take precedence. Not many balconies in Blighty. Spain and Italy are more like it. But media thrives. Dot-com companies abound. That's all that now matters.

Overt expressions of self-flattery have always been included in the gambits of amorous males. But, all considerations of ego aside, should not the obvious be asked? Has technology not latterly been responsible for elements of unabashed prurience entering into newly established forms of intercommunication? Has not the 'upload' and 'download' facility lured us into behaviour once deemed unthinkable but now perceived as quasi-acceptable? How do we measure social 'progress'? On what criteria may we define it – technological, moral? Behaviours and practices which are newly forged or without precedent, but which take root in public consciousness, be they subtle or audacious in their initial impact, are inevitably copied and repeated, gradually turning into convention. Few areas of contemporary life have remained unaffected by advances in computer technology or its encroaching application. And, as with many things, recently distorted notions of 'gallantry' have made their way into the domain of acceptable human conduct via the direct influence of technological change. Courtship ritual, or what's often described by social psychologists as 'pre-marital dating behaviour', has been overtaken by the technology of online social networking.

No longer are we governed by salutational niceties, decorum or any conception of *savoir vivre*. Where social interaction once provided the backdrop against which character could be developed, we have lost the sense of formality of occasion, and, with it, something of our civility. Gone are traditional rites of passage. Nor do we much concern ourselves over personal standards in quite the same way. Restraint, 'good form', nuances of tact, deportment, use of language, refined conduct of any sort seem to have lost value, their relevance as part of life's general education diminished with the removal of direct personal contact – via technology. Social discourse, it would seem, has been made meaningless, and arguably this is the web's greatest casualty. Most conversations are now unnecessary – superseded by email and text message, routinely rushed formats, the nature and circumstances of their use nearly always inattentive to grammar, vocabulary or the importance of correct spelling. The web cuts to the chase; the rest is noise. No need to talk; therefore, no need to cultivate the art of doing so.

Where meeting people is concerned, either professionally or socially, no longer do we need to feel excited expectation or the bitter-sweet mystery of anticipation. That the unique chemistry once created by personal interaction should now be lost as an unintended consequence of the digital age, speaks revealingly of the nature of progress. For all its merits in unleashing immense possibilities in the *efficiency* of communication, the computer, and our wholesale reliance upon it, has also brought its own peculiar example of the general failings of nearly all new technologies. Regard for any dimension of the human soul, i.e. that which makes us greater than the sum of our parts – temperament, sense of humour, delicacy of feeling, personality, sentiment, taste, aesthetic sense, intuition, sensibility, our capacity for emotional reaction – has been dispensed with as superfluous inconvenience. These traits have morphed into an equally abstract, *but entirely spiritless,* concern for cyberspace inclusion, involvement, complicity and erotology. Is it just possible we are producing a generation of screen-fixated geeks with diminished concentration spans and no social skills, but with an unnatural facility for pressing keys?

A computer is soulless. It makes 'decisions' by lightning-quick processes of reiterative calculation – algorithms – following formulaic, pre-programmed sets of instructions. A person, though also capable of calculation, makes a decision... by making a decision... with all the implications of both sagacity and misjudgement generally attributable to human meddling. In its designated standing within the nomenclature of new inventions, the computer's description *as 'computer'* accords it an accuracy of which no greater precision is possible. It's a machine that *computes*. Unlike a human being, it does not *intuit*. We can feel. We can make emotional decisions as well as cool, calculated, rational ones. Such a fundamental difference in the character of decision-making is what distinguishes us from any synthetic contraption. Endowed with *life,* a person has a brain, a heart, a sense of humour, a degree of passion and a moral compass. A computer has *software.* Not the same.

Direct engagement with people can now be reconstituted outside the constraints of time and space. Why the need to talk to anyone 'in the flesh' when you can more effortlessly do it on Skype? With the world 'Wi-Fied' and 'webcam-ed', why the need to arrange a date or rendezvous? Meeting in person? No need for a charm offensive! Just tap buttons; you needn't physically remove yourself from the comfort and convenience of your workstation. Social media sites are now the meeting points for humanity, our new matchmakers. Facebook and Twitter are our new public squares, cafes, cocktail bars, dance floors, pubs and nightclubs with their own formalities and rules of engagement. What's more, they are, in terms of capacity, the biggest such venues in history. With the idea of 'public domain' redefined, now often expressed in terms of 'cyberspace', the scale of social interaction is unprecedented. Yet, it would seem, no greater is the number of 'happy endings' as ever in the past.

Not long ago, people aged gracefully. Now they inject themselves with Botox at the faintest hint of facial wrinkles. The former was a natural process allowed to take its course. The latter is a manifestation of human vanity at its most narcissistic. Why look your age, when you could look younger? A natural propensity of human character perhaps. But for the self-absorbed, excessively modish or incurably bourgeois, immediate gratification, irrespective of long-term consequences, is perceived to be a preordained birth-right. So much so, that to sustain a synthetic image indefinitely, periodic reapplication of syringe and needle becomes a way of life, lest all facial flesh drops like melting wax. Can people delude themselves so completely? Yes, they can. We are a species capable of breath-taking folly, when blinded by conceit.

Once upon a time, having 'keyboard proficiency' simply meant you could play the piano. Now it means you're a computer geek. Rapid advances in technology have re-contextualised the generic meaning of non-technical terms and created subtle changes in the way we use standard English. Indeed the term 'geek' is a good example of a neologism, derived from Middle Low German, bearing the strikingly apt original meaning of *an odd person.* Likewise, 'clicking a mouse' may at one time have meant doing something unspeakable to a small rodent. A 'hard drive', up until the recent past, may well have described a difficult road journey. 'Google', as a derived word, was originally inspired by the utterances of a one-year-old child – by 'baby gibberish', that ungrammatical *abstraction of* language, spewed out by everyone between the ages of eight months and two years. Its prototype meaning was coined by the child's uncle, a mathematician, to denote a large number, specifically the quantity expressed by the numeral, one, followed by a hundred zeros. Entirely unrelated to information technology or computers, *google* was, rather, a term of reference originally belonging to a branch of pure mathematics, Number Theory. We cannot stop the slow evolution of how we speak; the social and cultural underpinnings, causally linked to 'usage', are far too strong. Nor is it necessarily desirable to tinker with the natural dynamic of a living language, something all too well understood by the Oxford English Dictionary Committee. We may now split the infinitive with impunity, without fear of committing an act of solecism or assaulting the integrity of grammatical correctness, all because of *usage*. The moral? Do something in the 'wrong' way long enough – persistently and pervasively enough – and it becomes accepted practice, slowly morphing into the 'right' way.

The implications of this persistence are far and wide, extending well beyond use of language or grammatical structures. So why not register your company in the Cayman Islands and minimise your tax liability to nearly nothing? Legally too! That such, and other, practices may leave one ethically bereft is a thought and sentiment of conscience either assuaged or exacerbated – *depending on individual moral character* – by its material trappings: the yacht, the Ferrari, the Bentley, the Cohibas, the fine vintage wines, the Canalettos. Living 'well' or 'stylishly', in itself, offers no grounds for accusations of wrongdoing or any form of improbity. The outsourcing of off-shore tax havens, as a means of protecting excessive corporate or individual wealth, falls entirely within the law. But the personal status and sense of self-importance fuelled by material success, the ego and affectation it nourishes, frequently morph into a defined lifestyle, a self-contained package, each element of which is related to the next, making it all too easy to lose awareness of distinctions between behaving 'morally' and behaving 'self-indulgently' *at the expense of others.*

The *bon viveur* and the jet-setting *nouveau riche* have always had a place in free societies, but they were never themselves free of the looming risks of such a lifestyle. Prodigious wealth has been known to ruin character. Lapsing into hedonism or delusions of grandeur, the fragility of will to resist transgressive temptations and the associated struggle for clarity of conscience are never far away. They are the scourges of 'high life', and examples abound.

If the staging of 'fundraisers' and social events in the service of charitable causes is to any extent an outward expression of repressed guilt, then ostentation can be said to have its merits: in delivering a sense of atonement and, at the same time, deftly expediting entitlement to tax concessions. Significantly, and paradoxically, it is such features as tolerance, acceptance, inclusiveness, diversity and openness that give society its appeal; and when extended to subsume all manner of dubious behaviour, including tax avoidance, it is only a mark of collective success. Such, at least, seems to be the prevailing perception among a large contingent of the entrepreneurial class, forcing on the remainder of society the cynical view that what we *see* is but a *representation* of what really *is*. That human behaviour is occasionally crafted for 'effect', and not consistently 'genuine', is just another reminder that there is no shortage of examples in life to confirm our general awareness of the intrinsic imperfections of the world. Differences between self-evaluation and how we are seen by others are an inescapable feature of living. Inevitably, throughout the course of a lifetime, there will be moments at which some of us will have committed what *others* may judge to be a 'moral' crime, though never once putting a foot outside man-made legislation. The blunt instrument of law, both civil and criminal, is an *objectification* of judgement – made to have *universal* application – whereas private judgement is wholly *subjective,* no more than individual opinion. As a commonly advanced argument, morality is *relative*, whereas public law, within its domain of jurisdiction, is *absolute.* That it is a practical impossibility to 'micro' legislate over 'fine' points of behaviour is not merely an indictment of how we live, but, in a larger sense, testament to the congenital nature of our moral limitations – for there are as many opportunities to act against the *spirit* of the law, within its *letter,* as there are legal loopholes. The human failing is that there is any necessity at all to draw distinctions between formal definitions of tax *avoidance* and tax *evasion*. Where the line between the two becomes subject to interpretation, obscured by deliberately vague or ambiguous legal wording, dishonesty is encouraged to run rampant. The very deed of straying *near* the threshold between avoidance and evasion casts a shadow of moral doubt irrespective of what is printed in statute books or in legislative acts. Iniquity gushes not at the point of *overstepping* defined legal limits, but well prior, where intention is exposed by *edging suspiciously close* to them. It would seem that humanity has always been conflicted between the merits of openness and transparency on the one hand and, on the other, orchestrating appearances so as to conceal the true nature of things. The flip-side of philanthropy can barely resist its own theatrics.

Modernity is a logical progression of everything preceding it and, as such, unavoidably rooted in the past. We are overwhelmed by the march of time, of all it brings us – both good and bad – and have little option but to live with it, at most, actively embracing it, at least, passively tolerating it. We must, one way or another, make an accommodation for it, if not full concession to it. Both individually and communally, people are agents of change – social, technological, moral – of the way we think and live. As responsible determinants of human progress, we function at the very interface between past and future, the present, an interactive confluence where the latest effects of human endeavour have been propelled by their causal antecedents from both the distant and immediate past.

It has been said that the past consists of memory, the future of expectation. But the present, which we inhabit, is an ever-moving shadow. It divides yesterday from tomorrow, and readily presents us with imponderables in our decision-making. Few of us, only the wisest among the human species, have had, throughout history, the capacity to be disenthralled of the darkness of 'now' to see the light of 'later' with any clarity. We fathom our misjudgements too late to correct their shortcomings or ill effects, thus embroidering our language with extenuating phrases like, "in retrospect ", "with the benefit of hindsight ", "it's easy to be wise after the event". Of course it is. What's hard is to be Socrates and to be wise to events *now, in the present*.

Examples are all too familiar. They are historic in scale and long-term consequences, yet at the same time, ordinary, so in front of us as to be overlooked.

Smoking cigarettes, as a diversion, a personal indulgence throughout the 1920's, '30's and '40's, made no adverse impact on the social values *of the day.* As a public activity, it was morally neutral, even glamorised by Hollywood, having, at the time, no *known* life-threatening association. How far we've come, and how thoroughly attitudes and public understanding have changed in the clear later light of confirmed causal links to all manner of lung disease and deadly illness.

There was a time when basic safety features in cars, such as seat belts, were considered unnecessary by both designers and manufacturers – the underlying assumption being that any responsible driver would ensure their superfluity. How consistently and perennially we've overestimated human judgement and general levels of driving competence, only to 'see the light' after thousands of preventable road fatalities. By all accounts, awareness of road safety had a slow start in relation to automobile mass production. In a world prior to health and safety law, or any formal notions of risk assessment and public welfare, it may well have been asked what it takes, to what extent outrages are allowed to ferment, before legislators, spurred by conscience, compel private interests to serve the public good. No doubt, such questions are always asked, yet corrective action always remains slow.

It was once thought impossible that heavier-than-air machines could fly, taken to be so as a matter of common sense. The principles of 'buoyancy' and 'mass-volume displacement', though known to man since the time of Archimedes, were historically misunderstood in the popular imagination. That a physical object of density greater than that of the medium in which it might be suspended could ever be a source of transport was dismissed for centuries as a fact of simple logic, where, in truth, it was a clear case of deluded intuition. For nearly the whole of recorded history, man was thought to be forever earthbound. Yet, no sooner had the science of applied aeronautics been developed to its full, than gone were our past 'certainties' and assumptions. When, a little over a generation after the Wright brothers, commercial airlines began raking in significant profits, the very memory of the impossibility of heavier-than-air flight was extinguished permanently; and a generation after that, humanity spectacularly escaped the earth's gravitational field altogether, to enable astronauts to walk on the moon. So much for being earthbound.

Many a truth is counter-intuitive, and many are the myths we live by. What do we *really* mean by 'common sense'? Is it not that which we intuit without examining? These, and other, distinct questions arise. What wrong-headed ideas are currently in practice by wider society, which will only be seen to be grossly mistaken in a hundred years' time? What is it we are doing *right now*, convinced we're being clever, that will make us look absurd before the century is out? Probably loads of things. We can't even imagine them... and that's the point. Enlightenment needs perspective. The 'now' is plagued with blind spots, which only the discoveries of 'later' can illuminate. Public attitudes change and behaviour adapts to accord with new conventional wisdoms – an inevitable outcome of ever-replenished, ever-modified knowledge *over time.*

But public understanding of scientific principles has always fallen short, ranging from the semi-accurate to the farcical. If asked, "what is gravity?" or "why is the sky blue?", few among the 'man in the street' would make reference to such as, "the force of attraction between two bodies of mass as defined by Newton's inverse square law" or "the effect of refraction, absorption and reflection of natural light from the sun when passing through the earth's atmosphere". But then, there's no reason to expect the man on the Clapham omnibus to have a technical grasp of any random area of specific knowledge. There is no legal or moral obligation for any of us to know how to cook a dish of 'Gnocchi alla Sorrentina', recommending with confidence and authority which wine best complements it, or how to dismantle a car engine and reassemble it to perfect working order. Unless we are physicists, Italian chefs or car mechanics, our ignorance in those fields is excusable. All of which highlights distinctions between specialist and general knowledge, and, significantly, the difference between practical application of acquired skill and academic understanding. But being convinced the earth is flat falls into quite another category. At various times in history, what passed as 'common knowledge' or universally acclaimed 'truth' spawned dangers potentially far greater than those of narrow interest, precisely because of its generality and the social implications of its widespread acceptance.

That the earth was ever anything but round or, more accurately, 'spherical' is perhaps the most striking example of historical misconstruction. Bertrand Russell, in his 1912 publication, *The Problems of Philosophy*, makes a distinction between knowledge by *acquaintance* and knowledge by *description*. The former consists of anything of which we have direct awareness, the world of appearances gleaned from 'sense data', physical objects we perceive in conscious experience, e.g., the colour and shape of the table at which I am sitting. The latter, *descriptive* knowledge, is based on an *evaluation* of the perceived phenomenon as *derived* from acquaintance, *not directly* experienced but *inferred* from sense data.

That we today all 'know' the earth to be spherical is based on description, *not* acquaintance. When, at the dawn of prehistory, primal man first looked out across the savannahs of east Africa, the panoramic views to have been witnessed were those of a flat surface. To have construed the horizon as convex in any way would have been unnatural, at odds with elementary perception. It was only at later stages of human development, with the application of inductive logic – reasoning from the specific to the general through a sequence of related observations – that any suggestion of global curvature became plausible. Beyond question, it was known to the Greeks that the earth was spherical in shape, the mathematician Eratosthenes actually calculating its circumference with remarkable accuracy.

Chapter 2
Do we *Really* Know...?

Doctrinaire views of the earth's flatness persisted throughout the Middle Ages, largely owing to institutional hegemony of thought and conscience by such as the Roman Catholic Church, usurping all claims of secular evaluation or humanist sentiment, and the inertia of an entire population's static complacency under its grip. The prevailing belief among the vast portion of an unlearned populace was at odds with scholars who argued that evidence showed the earth to be a sphere. It was an age intolerant of ideas arrived at by independent minds, outside the approbation of church authority. Petrarch and Dante made significant noises in suggesting that 'man is the measure of all things', not God, an irreverence later refined by Erasmus to better accord with the prevailing orthodoxy. Even prior to the Renaissance, William of Ockham, in a similar tenor of detraction for Church authority, gave us his 'razor', an important starting point for how 'induction' is correctly applied, without superfluous assumptions in reasoning from a specific observation to a drawn inference, each step of the procedure arrived at by rational *necessity* as opposed to *received* articles of faith, indoctrination or the extravagance of human whim. These were all subversive undercurrents, thinly veiled, to the period's dominant 'certainties' of religious belief, but they never posed a serious threat to the papacy. Neither humanism nor science stood a chance prior to the cataclysm of the Protestant Reformation, a vastly significant event establishing essential groundwork prerequisite to the liberation of the mind. Only then could evidence-based thought be allowed to flourish. It is no accident of chronology. That the Reformation preceded the Scientific Revolution was, rather, a case of indirect cause and effect. As two protracted events, the *sequence* in which they occurred was an absolute necessity of historical determinism. Our modern technological world is more indebted to the likes of Martin Luther than is generally understood or commonly appreciated.

Throughout history, much of what was once conventionally accepted has been replaced by its opposite. Columbus, derided for claiming he could reach the Far East by sailing west, was thought by some to be insane. No one's laughing now. Both Galileo and Copernicus suffered terribly at the hands of papal dogma. No one today would be brought to trial for evidence-based claims of a heliocentric solar system or that the earth is not best characterised as an 'immovable firmament'. No, the absurdity is now reversed. Light has fallen on the original, intuitive thought in each instance; so much for 'common sense' in all its unexamined blindness or the incorrigibility of 'eternal' truth. Today it is such as the Inquisition, and all it stood for, that's seen as a grotesque curiosity of history, an embarrassment of Western civilisation, not its accused.

And yet collective lessons of life, or practical wisdom, seldom have a lasting effect from one generation to the next. We invariably repeat the mistakes of history, suffering the full visceral impact of their consequences before truly appreciating the meaning of both our thought and action. It's hardly an irrelevance today that one of the recurring themes of ancient Greek tragedy is "man attains wisdom through suffering". Aeschylus, Sophocles and Euripides understood that nothing is learned from past failings without having, ourselves, experienced horror, blood, fear, grief, anguish. We learn through active engagement, by the living reality of personal experience, but only when accompanied by distress and torment. Without these, it's a near impossible feat of imagination or emotion to accomplish anything worthwhile in effecting internal change. We don't *get it* till it hurts. Wisdom is but healed pain.

Socrates showed what it truly means to *know* something, how to question that which is conventionally accepted, pointing out that a good deal of what we commonly take to be unassailably true is riddled with flaws and biased preconceptions. The ancients understood the vital distinction between mere 'information' and 'knowledge' – knowledge as an evaluation of perception and as inference tested against *observable* fact – further demonstrating that 'to know' is essentially unattainable in any quest for absolute certainty or 'objective' truth. To a hitherto superstitious world, Socrates introduced rationalism. Yet, the received 'wisdom' of myths and gods persisted alongside great strides in the development of scientific methodology. It was in classical antiquity that the *way* in which knowledge is determined was made formal, *methodical,* for the first time in human culture. Aristotle, in his seminal works on the natural sciences, *Physics, Metaphysics, Prior Analytics, Posterior Analytics* and *On the Heavens,* set out rigorous procedures by which hypotheses were drawn from empirical observation. As generative writings emerging from what came to be acknowledged as the earliest civilisation with identifiably 'Western' or

European characteristics – where *theory,* as knowledge *for its own sake*, superseded *application* – these works were the historical source by which formal logic came to be utilised in producing a scientific account of nature. The Greeks were beginning to objectify the world, to *consciously* interpret it in terms that could be *universally* understood, laying the foundation of scientific enquiry as the only means by which knowledge may have any validity or legitimate claim to truth. Doing so, moreover, was a tacit acknowledgement, for the first time in world civilisation, that the *process* by which conclusions are reached cannot be separated from the nature of the *conclusion* itself – the *rigour* of the former determining the *soundness* of the latter. Means and ends are inseparable. The 'medium', as it were, *is* the 'message'.

But, as Hume convincingly argued, reason is the slave of passion; the irrational component of human constitution – of mind and spirit – often seems to prevail over calculated judgement, and Christianity interrupted the advancement of evidence-derived knowledge until the scientific revolution of the late seventeenth century. In one of the great dialogues of Plato, *Theaetetus*, the eponymous character, engages with Socrates, in the established dialectic of question and answer, over the direct point, "What is knowledge?" The result thrown up is essentially reducible to "true belief" and "an account" of it – effectively, an evaluation of perception. By the essence of their meaning, 'evaluation' and 'perception' are, respectively, commutable to *rationalism* and *empiricism,* formal schools of thought which emerged at that later stage in the history of Western philosophy, the hundred and fifty years from Descartes in the early-mid 1600's to Hume in the age of enlightenment at the end of the eighteenth century.

That this came in the wake of, not prior to or contemporaneous with, the Reformation is consistent with any understanding of *causation,* the linkage of one historical event with another and the necessary sequence in which they occur. The specific case of radical ecclesiastical reform in the early sixteenth century, *followed by* rapid development in secular philosophy and science stands as an elegant demonstration of how inspired changes at the root of institutional practices and organised structures of traditional belief can prevail upon thought processes on a widespread scale, doing nothing less than redirecting the course of history. The Protestant Reformation, as instigated by Martin Luther, sparked off a century and a half of religious turmoil. In his dissent over the sale of papal 'indulgences', Luther did more than he knew. His central claim was that there is nothing in Holy Scripture to support the practice of absolution of sin through declarations made by *ecclesiastical hierarchy*. The means to salvation is, instead, through an individual's simple faith, and the Vatican's widespread practice of atonement through confession, as part of the sacrament of penance, *offered through monetary payment* was not only innately vile and scandalous, it was an abuse encouraging *greed*, itself a deadly sin. By the simple act of posting his written protestations onto the door of the Castle Church, Wittenberg on the eve of All Saints' Day, 31st October 1517, Luther set in motion an unstoppable dynamic of history.

The Reformation was the Continent's most profound convulsion in the millennium succeeding the fall of imperial Rome in the West. As a robust and concerted reaction against a tainted central authority, it rapidly evolved into a movement that sprouted a variety of sects, locked in sustained disputation over fundamental church doctrine, lasting well into the following century, resolving, in time, into full schism with the Holy See. And as the Renaissance – the revival of 'the Classical Heritage' which had reached the north Italian city states a century earlier – was now beginning to infiltrate north of the Alps, continental Europe was to rouse itself out of the slumber of medievalism and into early modern times. In no small measure, this transformation was to be abetted materially by commercial success in trade, but even more so by the changed mentality incited through moral outrage at the long-accumulated excesses of a corrupt papacy. For all the religious strife following 1517, the eventual assimilation of Protestantism into the European legacy of Christian faith was to have an incalculable bearing on the subsequent cultural and intellectual development of the West.

By the mid-seventeenth century, the whirlwind of Luther's Reformation had largely dissipated, having culminated in formal settlement after the Thirty Years War with the Peace of Westphalia (1648), establishing Protestantism – and, crucially, a certain *independence of mind* that came with it – as an integral part of the fabric of European faith and culture. The religious complexion of Europe was recast and redefined, the rise of a new order of sovereign nation states replacing an outdated bent for loyalty to Rome. It was in the spirit of such change – in questioning dogma, in doctrinal separation, in redirecting allegiances and, vitally, in the cultural shift brought about by acknowledging the need for constitutional balance between individual liberty of conscience and central authority – that a reformed and revitalised religious sensibility quickly translated into a new civic and political consciousness throughout significant swathes of northern and central Europe. The ensuing effect on mass psychology, whereby liberated thought, no longer burdened by official tenet or autocratic institutions, created the milieu for tolerance and independence of mind. As the dominant source of concentrated power in Europe, the Vatican had had its day. And, as a revolution in human consciousness, the Protestant Reformation had become something profoundly more consequential than the mere ecclesiastical reform of its original design. It had taken on a force of its own.

This sense of liberation resonating from the spirit of Wittenberg was, by the start of the eighteenth century, to give impetus to prolific advancements in both enlightened political theory and 'the new science'. Through a sustained dialectic of volatile and reactive events, with origins traceable to Luther, and which were to have far-reaching social and political ramifications on individual liberty, meritocracy and democratic conceptions of a free society – from the Glorious Revolution of 1688 to the French Revolution of 1789 – Europe was decidedly 'going secular'. Voltaire's remark about the Holy Roman Empire, "... it wasn't holy, it wasn't Roman and it wasn't an empire", was in no sense to have remained unsubstantiated. Only peripherally ever 'Roman' at the furthest stretch of its southern geographical extremity, the Holy Roman

Empire, if anything, was predominantly Austro-Germanic. Hardly an 'empire', it was a decentralised patchwork of autonomous principalities, independent city states, self-governing duchies and petty buffer zones. As for 'holy', divisive conflict with Catholic doctrine and denunciation of the moral failings of the papacy had grown to be its defining features since the pre-Protestant martyrdom of Jan Hus, over a century prior to Luther. Moreover, disputes between emperors and popes over the issue of 'investiture', on who had the authority to appoint bishops or depose kings, had been almost continuous since the eleventh century. The Reformation further weakened the empire's internal bonds as divisions between Protestant and Catholic regions took on emotive new definition. But by 1650 both philosophy and science had, at long last, solid new ground, free of religious dogma, on which to advance in leaps and bounds. And, beginning with the prodigious achievements of Descartes, Leibniz and Newton, they did.

The quintessential rationalists, Descartes, Spinoza and Leibniz, all presented ideas which were to flourish from the mid-seventeenth century; the great empiricists, Locke, Berkeley and Hume, did the same a little later. But it was Immanuel Kant, later still, who, in his defining work, *Critique of Pure Reason,* is credited with the fusion of rationalism and empiricism as a self-contained procedure in the quest for certainty. Empiricism alone – that's to say, experience, observation, sensation and perception – cannot complete the entire mechanism necessary for scientific method to function fully. But integration with rationalism, i.e., the application of *inductive* and *deductive* logic to empirical observation, makes the method whole. Plato had the nub of it. In saying that knowledge is an evaluation of perception, he was saying that what we 'know' is determined by logic applied to observation; he was defining an area of confluence between 'belief' and 'truth'.

Yet, 'science', as a formally structured and rigorously defined method of enquiry, complete with philosophical underpinnings, free of all inkling of superstition, did not come to its historical fruition until the end of the eighteenth century – over two millennia after its initiation in classical antiquity, in the Athens of Plato and Aristotle, around 350 BC. By this measure, it could reasonably be argued that Christianity has much to answer for, stalling the development of science for some sixteen centuries. Emotion-driven evaluation can, by all accounts, be said to have assumed historically epic proportions in every instance of the world's major religious faiths. To this day, the human tendency for blind unquestioning acceptance continues to survive the triumph of science, running in parallel with it, however absolute the latter's predominance over contemporary civilisation. As a species, we are truly curious creatures, capable of reason yet fundamentally subject to the influence of passion, an abstraction governed by a 'logic' all its own, originating in some ill-understood realm of the subconscious mind. By every indication, Hume was right.

Computer 'geekery' is not knowledge *per se*, but rather, knowledge *dependent*. It is predicated on honed skills necessary to draw up 'information' through proficient familiarity with pressing keys on a board. 'Information' is not knowledge, but sterile assertion, which may be true or not, quantitative and finite in character. It is radically unlike the qualitative nature of 'knowing' as characterised by understanding, objective evaluation, a disciplined capacity for critical thinking, informed assessments on the basis of tangible evidence and the application of inductive logic in drawing generalised inferences from specific observations. There exists no other accredited procedure by which to formulate a universal theory or, at least, a plausible explanation of any phenomenon in the natural world subject to human perception.

And yet, the entire enterprise of seeking 'to know' is infused with uncertainty – as the only enduring certainty. That our senses can be deceived, that our capacity to reason can lead us to self-contradiction, paradox and all manner of logical conundrum speaks volumes of the intrinsic imperfection of both empiricism and rationalism. Interpretations of sense data and logical progressions by association, whether causal or correlative, from self-evident premises are problematical. The very nature of 'inference' and 'induction', of generalising on foundations, is little more than educated guesswork, making the whole of human knowledge tentative, never complete, never final. Why? Because there can be *more than one* 'rational necessity' that follows a specific premise. In Western scientific tradition, it is generally the simplest explanation that is taken as being closest to the truth (Occam's razor). But at the same time we cannot be assured that any such choice is the *only* 'simplest' one. And therein lies the implicit weakness of induction. Theories require ongoing modification so as to accommodate 'counter-examples' as revealed through trials of practical application. Always subject to being made more concise and inclusive, long-standing theories, when tested against the measurable quantities of scientific experimentation, are forever being amended, updated, finely tuned in the light of fresh evidence or new angles of explanation. By virtue of being subject to falsifiability, theories are endlessly being made 'leaner' and 'truer'. That, itself, is an indication that certainty of knowledge can only be approached, not reached; the path to certainty is a pursuit, a perpetual quest, never allowing us to arrive at a settled version of the truth. In this, its *lack of finality*, knowledge may best be characterised as *qualitative, not quantitative*, a dynamic *process* without end. And if the only methodologies we can ever hope to develop for determining knowledge are, of necessity, flawed, it follows that 'to know' is reducible to personal *conviction* as rooted in *belief,* which is, in turn, subjective, not universally identifiable, understood or shared.

The difficulty in any attempt at arriving at an assured or comprehensive 'theory of truth' may be seen in the disorder that arises from the sheer variety and character of ideas put forth concerning it and the ongoing debates between their contrasting schools of thought. Metaphysical 'realists' suggest that a statement is 'true' only if it accurately corresponds, or is 'isomorphic', to structures observable in the physical world. 'Idealists' argue that *all* existence is ultimately in the mind and, as such, correlation between claims of truth and direct perception can never be convincingly validated outside the limits of the mind's capacity for interpreting the physical world. Yet another, historically recent, line of enquiry is that of the 'linguists', part of the twentieth-century school of 'logical positivism', now widely discredited, which emphasises little beyond an analysis of the structures and properties of language in determining the truth of anything observed or imagined. Such diffracted and divergent strands of thought over the nature of truth makes a single cohesive theory impossible; all of which leaves us with the disquieting thought that there simply is no such thing as *objective* truth, except perhaps as the hypothetical *aggregate of all subjective* evaluations. That, to this day, such disparate and conflicting points of argument should endure demonstrates the inherent limitations in reasoning from the specific to the general. The built-in flaw of inductive logic and its application is best exposed by a circularity readily seen when defining *knowledge* as the confluence of *belief* and *truth*; belief derives from nothing more than *subjective* conviction, and truth is unknowable except as 'particular' judgement, beyond our grasp outside the realm of individual perception, not uniquely definable in terms of a *universal* ideal. As a methodology for arriving at reliable conclusions, induction barely leaves us any closer to understanding what it means 'to know' or being able to identify that which is 'true'.

Can we ever claim to really know, *with certainty*, anything at all? The rationalists, on the bedrock of Descartes, may assure us that we are each 'a thing that thinks', for in doubting that we're doubting... we're doubting – *engaging in mental activity* – therefore, we can be *certain of some kind of conscious existence*. 'Cartesian doubt', which began an entire school of thought – logically self-contained and indispensable as a component of scientific procedure – has had profound and wide-ranging implications in *epistemology,* the theory of knowledge itself. In being certain of our capacity to think, *if nothing else,* we are justified in claiming our existence, hence the Cartesian cogito, "I think, therefore I am".

The empiricists, on the other hand, in support of *certainty,* would, in all likelihood, level the argument for *phenomenology* – that when we perceive something, anything tangible, we needn't fuss unduly over dubious assumptions about the nature of its existence. We can be *certain* of its existence *as an object of perception,* irrespective of the notion that it may just be a *representation* of reality, rooted in some *noumenal* realm of the mind or in an *ideal* world beyond space and time, impervious to our understanding of it as a *thing in itself.* This notion, famously dating from Plato's *Forms,* was, in the seventeenth century, not entirely new; *but* it was arrived at from a fresh starting point, independent of its historical provenance, *and further developed* as a dominant school of thought over the following one hundred and fifty years.

Kant's view would have squared with this, and taken it further. As an 'ontological idealist', he may well have suggested that the nature of human *physiology* and the apparatus provided by our sensory organs are such as to *predispose* us to a particular configuration or 'mapping' of the physical world. This limits our capacity for evaluating perceptible objects to a scrutiny of mere 'representations' of the mind, their ultimate reality unknown. It is an empirical line of thought in subject-object relations with elements of rationalism employed in arriving at its conclusion. The trouble is that both rationalist and empiricist approaches are limited precisely by this finite capacity of human physiology. We cannot break out of the innate limits imposed by our own wherewithal – a notion which, perhaps, delineates the outer boundaries of all that can be meant by 'knowledge'. And if the news is not quite as bad as to say, *we don't know anything*, it would not be unreasonable to suggest that the means at our disposal for arriving at *certain* knowledge is eminently imperfect.

The human capacity for rational thought, as posited by Kant, is built into the fabric of sensation and perception, also incorporating our intuitive faculty for understanding delineations of *time*, three-dimensional *space* and *causal relations*. Rationalism, in effect, is rooted in empiricism. This notion was elaborated by

Schopenhauer, who proposed that Kant was correct up to that point, but departed from the next step of his insight by suggesting that anything purely noumenal, outside experience and perception, cannot admit of such distinctions or configurations as time and space. The nature by which we make rational interpretations of sense data, by one-to-one correspondence between subject and object – the mind lending meaning to what the eye observes – is *particular* to the observer and cannot truly be objectified or evaluated in terms that are universally understood. Specific cases of perception can never be tenable or in any way conceptualised in the metaphysical realm outside experience, where all is *undifferentiated* and where there exists no concept of, or basis for, the relevance of *time,* Euclidean *space* or *cause and effect.* In our conscious state of being, we observe material objects only within time and space, the logic employed in any evaluation of their nature not extending beyond the realm of the mind. Our being is, effectively, one and the same as the palpable structures of space and time, wherein the cosmos as a whole is contained in individual consciousness. Remove the person, i.e., remove the phenomenal world of appearances – of space, time and causality *which lie within us* – and the entire universe also disappears. We are, according to Schopenhauer, left with cosmic *will.* Perception and its concomitant structures of time and space are created only through our own conscious existence. They are *within us* and do not stand apart from us. It is in this sense that rationalism is 'subservient' to empiricism, as Hume would have had it. And, as developed by Kant, with a later adaptation by Schopenhauer, this conception of what is *real* became the essence of 'metaphysical idealism' by which all mental processes, thought and perception, are but representations of the mind. There is no *external* reality.

An intriguing counterpart, or updated variant, of this line of thought might best be encapsulated by Sartre's notion that *existence precedes essence*. Where the empiricist may proclaim, "The world is *as I see it*", the rationalist would rephrase the same idea as "I see the world *as it is*". But the existentialist view, where free will and individual existence are central to *everything*, would tend to override both claims by declaring, "The world is *nothing, until I say anything about it*".

Leibniz, by the start of the eighteenth century, had made the distinction between the 'rational' and 'empirical' as two divergent types of derived knowledge, using terminology of his own invention, though for an established dichotomy belonging to a tradition with origins in classical antiquity. What he termed 'analytic', or *a priori,* knowledge is that determined without reference to the external world or to observation, but, rather, worked out solely in the mind on the basis of self-evident axioms aided by calculation, inductive or deductive; for example: '2+3=5'. It is an 'internal' process, *rational* in character. 'Synthetic', or *a posteriori*, knowledge is that acquired by drawing inferences from direct perception of phenomena in the physical world of experience, e.g., 'grass is green', 'fire is hot', 'water is wet' and so forth. It is 'external' and *empirical* in character. As yet another interesting twist, the modern existentialist view of this is, effectively, that conscious awareness, itself, takes precedence over all and every human compass for making any such appraisal – analytic *or* synthetic, rational *or* empirical. These are purposeless exercises of hair-splitting distinctions and of idle concern in the light of such matters as 'existence', 'free will' and 'extinction'. Pre-empting both rationalism and empiricism, the existentialist mind shifts the emphasis to 'being', in the absence of which there is simply 'nothingness', neither anything noumenal, of the mind, nor material, of the observable world.

Chapter 3
Floating on the Past

But, so what? Why is having any inkling of this either necessary or important? Of what relevance, it might be asked, is the history of formal thought processes dating from antiquity to how we think and live today? In the final analysis, it makes little difference to individual well-being or to the potential for personal happiness. Yet, the least that may be said is that, even in the most practical sense of living, it *can* be useful to know. The history of thought is the history of abstractions but the independent variable determining its worth, whether perceived as significant or trifling, is *mental* attitude. Philosophy offers no solutions. It opens up paths to understanding or, rather, the best *attempt* at understanding as allowed by human wit. Needless to say, it is in comprehending the nature of what it means 'to know' that we may be best equipped to assess everything around us –

observing, making judgements, drawing conclusions, taking decisions, be they life-changing or trivial. The importance of knowledge consists not only in its direct practical utility, but also in its all-important side effect, that of promoting a contemplative habit of mind: the means, the medium, the process, the methodology of thinking. Our capacity to question the merits of *how we live* can only be sharpened by all that is to be availed of the past; for there is a useful link to be made between the history of ideas and contemporary ideas of lifestyle – by a carefully selected adaptation from one to the other. Our comprehension of modernity, our very conception of it, and all its associations, would be vastly diminished without a sense of the tradition out of which arises the manner and approach by which we identify relationships between one idea and another, as decision-making parameters. A sense of past, present and future, a grasp of causality, of how one event is related to the next, both in substance and in sequence, within the framework of time, shapes and informs our current concerns and future expectations. It is an insight prerequisite to understanding the essence of modernity – of *how we live,* now. Our way of life has a rationale that supports it, assumptions that underlie it, and it exerts subconscious influences of which we are, by definition, barely aware. These have grown into the fabric of modern life and are underpinned by historic superstructures within which we think and function, overwhelming influences we cannot readily see in isolation as they form all-pervasive backdrops to current life, to *the way we live*: technology, industrialisation, commercialisation and mass media.

To understand modernity, the 'here and now' in which we are immersed, the first allusion must be to the vast past which elevates us to the present. The specific junctures in time at which dramatic and decisive events take place – where 'cause' produces 'effect' – form a long continuous strand of points at which two antithetical ideas collide and synthesise to propel forward the narrative of history. It is a known dynamic (Hegel's dialectic) which has brought us to the present, to our familiar plight and how we perceive it, enabling us to forge our values. That we are slow to exploit the precious availability of all that can be gained by delving into the past is an oversight of which we are often culpable, of not permitting ourselves to look back in wonderment at the richness of lessons to be learned and sources of inspiration. The conduct and character of contemporary life has a traceable lineage. Our values, concerns and priorities have lines of relevance leading back to socio-historical beginnings. And looking at major historical waves of events and how they might be related, in reverse chronological order, can be an insightful exercise in 'causation'. Connections seem to come to light with unexpected clarity, however oversimplified. We might ask, for instance:

Would *the way we live* today have been the same were it not for multinational corporations and the technology they have made commercially available? Would technology have been possible without science, industry and big business? Would democracy and capitalism, as politically and socially crafted mechanisms for wealth creation in a free society, have developed to the same extent as they have without industrialisation? Would the Industrial Revolution have gained traction with such accelerated strides as at the start of the nineteenth century without the extraordinary advances of the scientific revolution of the previous century and a half? Would science, from the late seventeenth century to date, have developed at the same pace, or have had the same far-reaching effects, without a religious reformation prior to its resurgence with a resultant abrogation of dogmatic belief? Would the Reformation have assumed any significant vigour without the growing influence, in the late fifteenth and early sixteenth centuries, of humanism and the Renaissance? Would the Renaissance have been at all possible without the 'Classical Heritage', the ancient legacies of Greece and Rome?

Cause and effect leap out; the links and associations, when paraded before us, seem all too graphic. *That we enjoy our smartphones, Socrates debated ideas in the Agora*... Far-fetched? Not when subject to analysis. The greater the detail in which we examine causal links, the more plausible becomes the specific direction of the tide of world events. While any reconstruction of the past is always subject to interpretation and is sometimes conjectural, understanding 'modernity' is nothing more than a grasp of 'the connections' of history and keeping up with the pace of change. That the starting point of the modern age has been designated and identified as having originated from the beginning of the sixteenth century is far from arbitrary. The discovery of new continents and trade routes, coupled with the Renaissance and the Reformation, left Europe with the groundwork for a lasting legacy of institutional structures which today define *the way we live* and all that makes us 'modern': democracy, applied science, capitalism, national identity and globalisation.

Chapter 4
Eternal Ends... Changing Means

All is flux, as the ancients well understood. Each generation comes of age with ever-changing social values. But each fresh wave of humanity seems to have an unchanging need for emotional sanctuary. Some find it in the creative and performing arts; others, in any number of self-indulgences – extravagance of one description or another, from recreational 'substances' to extreme sport. Quite apart from the travails of career and work, their related stress and the disciplines associated with relieving it, people seem to need diversion as a counterbalance to the tedium of reality, developing defence mechanisms against the pressures of the competitive struggle implicit in mere existence, if not wholesale repugnance of the horrors of the world. We occasionally turn to practical applications of Eastern philosophies, to such as Zen Buddhism or yoga meditation techniques, with varying degrees of success, ever hopeful of achieving 'inner peace' amidst the chaos around us or physiological and muscular control of our own bodies. Many of us benefit from concessionary company rates to fitness centre membership. But where the merits of physical stamina and worldly comforts fail us, or the putative virtues of Wall Street and the City fall short of expectation, we inevitably find alternative ways of punctuating our lifestyle, adding to it a touch of colour and variety, a 'thrill' or seditious 'kick', as redress for lack of fulfilment of one kind or another, usually aesthetic or emotional, occasionally material or visceral.

Now, for the first time in human history, it is possible to be comprehensively stupefied by a computer screen, and, what's more, to be so affected in a better informed, more fulfilling way than by any predated means. So, why listen to a Mahler symphony in its totality when you could download excerpts of it from a variety of memorable performances, enabling a comparison of interpretations by different conductors? Why read a Shakespeare play in full when you could conveniently tap out 'sound bites' of his best lines or a synopsis of any one of his works, with critical analyses of plot and character? For that matter, why opt for a gin and tonic? Indeed, why indulge in any number of sensate recreations, on either side of legality, when you can be mesmerised to a far greater stress-relieving outcome, legally, with the merits of browsing through a virtually unlimited choice of all the information ever accumulated by humanity?

These are but a few examples of 'traditional' behaviour as contrasted with, and largely supplanted by, their counterpart in the modern digital age. Every latest generation has its own 'take on life', on achieving, or seeking to manage, the same eternally desired ends humanity judges to be worth pursuing or the necessity of primitive drives and biological survival instinct compels us to consummate. It is only the means to such ends which change, largely owing to new technologies – an enticement to question whether there really *is* any such thing as 'modernity'. Rather, it would seem that each generation fashions fresh versions of old ideas, recycled over centuries, adapted to suit – and sometimes define – not only morals and manners but conceptions of lifestyle *of the day*, in all their transitory currents of fashion and modishness.

Such ideas of *how we should live* are as eternal as any basic human need, but their application is always new, continually replenished, the technology of the moment making the ideas topical or fashionable, and, when coupled with personal preference, determining the specific nature of their deployment. There was never a time in history, for instance, when we, as a species, didn't care to listen to music in a concentrated way. We have done so in all manner of contexts and for a diversity of reasons and motivations: simple enjoyment, public festivals, private concerts, liturgical church services, social or entertainment events, ceremonies, emotional therapy, cinematic or theatrical accompaniment, historical or academic interest. But we have also done it through hugely varied *media* throughout time: 'streaming', pod-cast, CD, cassette tape, LP, radio broadcast and, of course, live performance. Technology has produced endless such listening 'formats', but before Edison first recorded and reproduced sound at the end of the nineteenth century, the only way to experience music, for millennia, was 'live'. It was the original listening 'context' – not 'format', for lack of intervening *medium* – and, by definition, will always remain the most natural and purest way of listening. This can only be attributable to the age-old idea of music's charm and delight, serving congenital human tastes which fundamentally stand *outside* any need for technology or artificial contrivance. And, as a specific example, it demonstrates the enduring relationship between means and ends. In the rendition of music and, by extension, most forms of art, any 'synthetic' means of delivery which stands between content and reception, be it aural or visual, will inevitably diminish the full effect of the composer's or artist's intention. When music is produced 'live', on instruments historically evolved and devised for its specific 'idiom', it is expressed in 'puristic' form. When recorded and 'regurgitated' through some device, it creeps into our ears with a different connotation – impure, electronically affected, manipulated by engineers in a recording studio. Adaptations of means change. Eternal truths remain. Likewise, face-to-face human contact bears a similar comparison with any exchange as imparted and received by the intervention of that third element, the *medium*.

Cyberspace, as an alternative reality, has thus encroached upon every field of life; it's used for everything, not only for tapping into sources of useful information via powerful search engines. It serves the full range of human goals, obsessions, aspirations, preoccupations – be they necessary or superfluous. It allows us to fulfil them, to convert abstract intention into practical action, however diverse its scope and range, however varied its gravitas or triviality. New rules of expediency have opened up for everything from entrepreneurship and wealth creation to reserving theatre seats, purchasing airline tickets, booking hotel rooms or playing solitaire. We can now carry out nearly any personal banking transaction without having to trek to our high-street branch. We can arrange a 'package tour', catch up with missed broadcasts and films; we can find a partner for life or just a 'quick fling', all entirely to our preference and within stride of our personal pace of living. In its utility and sheer convenience, the computer is almost guilt-inducing. It is effortless to 'download' and fill in all kinds of application form and send them off with remarkable dispatch, conduct interviews 'on screen', translate documents and articles, look up arcane definitions, place an order for the purchase of nearly *any* product or service. We can record and produce our own self-made music, setting up a marketing and sales website for it. Who needs EMI, Polygram or Decca anymore? With the very concept of a 'recording industry' outdated, and erstwhile corporate efforts at mass-marketing and promotion reduced to 'uploading', 'downloading' and 'streaming', we've all morphed into self-publicising commercial entities. Letter writing, though largely superseded by email, may, nevertheless, still be affected *by the very instrument which has changed it* – with the simple function of 'print'. Quite a marvel, that we may engage in any form of literary enterprise or academic research with the same tool that allows us to pay our utility bills, order groceries or prepared meals for delivery to our doorstep, hire a babysitter or view a missed episode of *Fawlty Towers*.

Name *anything* – any wild, random assortment of pedestrian human activities or practical concerns -- from tips on how to correctly apply facial make-up to searching for the best deal on car insurance, solving chess puzzles, booking Eurostar to Paris, studying the design plans of the Titanic, shopping at Waitrose, taking tea at Claridge's, applying probability theory to quantum mechanics, cooking a dish of 'Linguine Gamberoni' or getting to Ilford on the No. 25 bus – any area of life – and our first point of engagement with it is in thinking of how we can *use our computer to do it.* Of goods and services, products and processes, every imaginable consumer need has gone 'online'. 'Uber' and 'App' economies have been created, whereby, if carried to their logical extreme, anybody can do or become anything at any time. From my bedroom, I could claim to be a taxi service, a recording company, my own publisher, a set designer for Broadway musicals – you name it – all reducible to tapping buttons, clicking, scrolling and CGI-ing. The world's gone 'facile'. If trained in nearly any skill or craft, you need little more than your laptop to make a profession of it.

But doing so, both incidentally and controversially, can imperil traditional structures and practices of long-established industries, diluting standards of professionalism. That London cabbies have little reason to be fond of Uber is yet another reminder, at its most poignant, of the casualties of new technology. For 'the knowledge' of London streets and one-way systems to have been replaced by tapping buttons in the crass, incompetent manner we have witnessed is nothing short of outrageous, unthinkable only a few years ago. The hackney cab, since the days of its earliest incarnation as the horse-drawn hansom carriage, has been strongly identifiable with Britain – much as red telephone boxes, policing by public consent as opposed to visible force of arms, 'greasy spoon' cafes, fish and chip shops and pubs, iconic features and practices of British civic life. And for all of these, there is now much muted concern. If either public service or commercial considerations are to overtake cultural and traditional ones, it is widely felt that any form of immediate advantage or cost-effectiveness *at the price of* blighting the character of a national institution is, in the long-term, false economy.

Well, perhaps... but almost certainly not in all instances. The issue is reducible to generational differences in *sentimental value*. Of images and symbols, customs and conventions, once staunchly part of national identity, desirable and constructive, now subject to slow disappearance, there are distinctions to be made among them, over the organic endurance of their tenure and the natural cause of their slow extinction.

"To everything there is a season", as was said three thousand years ago. There comes a time at which technological innovation puts paid to the social necessity of all products, services and processes as once used, applied and practised. When public demand finds new directions through modernisation, a point of diminishing returns is reached, at which change is due, sensible and economically expedient. Public telephone boxes are now obsolescent in every practical sense, modern telephony, the smartphone, having literally made museum pieces of them. And while pining for specific features of times past sometimes gives way to sentimentality, the newly arisen *need* for change always, in the last analysis, embodies its own compelling justification even in the minds of hardened traditionalists. Progress and modernity go nowhere without calm, rational judgement prevailing over sentiment. They override all enticements to 'look back' – especially for the *incoming* generation. *Sentimental value* is an expense incurred only by the *outgoing* one.

Traditional black cabs, though subject to gradual vanishing, appear to be doing so at a far slower pace than red telephone booths. Software developers would be hard put to replace Cockney humour and 'the gift of the gab'. Apart from the need to reconfigure pricing structures for greater competitiveness, there is little cause for the demise of the hackney cab, *as yet*. But, by mid-century, so our visionary pundits predict, digital, *driverless*, electronically powered vehicles, instantly programmable to convey passengers from any given postcode to any other, will rapidly precipitate the swansong of both the traditional cab and the business concept of Uber. Like death and taxes, obsolescence via technology is an inevitability of life.

In much the same way, the prominence of print journalism has been vastly diminished by new technologies, while such damaging phenomena as 'fake news' and all manner of disinformation have been made possible in ways far more menacing than in the past. Social media companies have yet to find an effective means of filtering out the malicious from the acceptable in the lifeblood of their industry, information. The future belongs to regulation, the implications for democracy and free societies, profound.

Social change is, indeed, traceable to necessity. It is intended and calculated for practical use toward the attainment of ends serving unchanging needs. From one generation to the next, this application assumes a more 'advanced' means of reaching those ends. And, in the course of so doing, new perceptions, fresh approaches in mental attitude and transient consumer values are bound to arise as natural by-products, affecting society in immediate and profound ways. Improvement in technology and its social dissemination through effective marketing by big business assumes, over time, a repetitive pattern by which we recycle the same stuff – the same agency serving human need – only in a different way, under the guise of new formats, believing them to be an improvement on the past. Obsolescence takes place largely in the mind. A product or service is gradually attenuated of its efficacy *only in relation to* an innovative replacement which out-competes it in both commercial viability and technological efficiency. Every familiar accessory of life is subject to such termination and disappearance. That which stays behind, and always endures, becomes an abstract 'texture' of day-to-day concerns as driven by the pursuit of basic human need. It survives all forms of external change by making an accommodation for such change, adjusting to innovation and improvement. As part of a larger vanishing world, the fading features of an identifiably British way of life may often stir our sentiment. But the past always continues to survive in the mind, and sooner or later we all come to see that that which replaces the once familiar opens up new possibilities and areas of interest, giving us something better suited to purpose. We adapt to the 'new' while developing sentimental attachment to the 'old', eventually realising that what we *really* miss is the *means*, not the *end* – the iconography and its clinging associations, its *representational value as opposed to* its *functionality*.

We are left with ever fewer route masters, red phone boxes, family-run 'chippies', 'greasy spoons', post offices, 'bobbies on the beat', black cabs. But these are predictable effects of the unyielding tide of progress. We've come a long way from *Dixon of Dock Green* as a standard image of the English policeman – without really pausing to think that, *even in its own day*, it was a larger-than-life portrayal of reality. And, however wistful we might grow through our tendency to idealise the past, we are, at the same time, aware that progress is of our own making and volition. We acknowledge, be it expressly or tacitly, that moving forward is both natural and necessary. As practical realities, the frills and paraphernalia of the present must, of necessity, recede into the past and remain irretrievable. We will always want, at any given moment in history, better, more efficient, less time-consuming ways of getting from one place to another, improved means of communicating, better ways of being informed, educated, protected, nourished, sheltered, rested, entertained, enlightened. The need is eternal, the manner of reaching it, new and ever changing. Modernity consists of nothing more than innovative means to unchanging ends.

We are already seeing the beginnings of doing all these things in ways that are increasingly 'paperless', 'driverless', energy efficient. Ever-innovative software, 'smart' technology and artificial intelligence will allow us to achieve goals undreamt of in the past. We are all naturally drawn to the marvels of the latest technology. But, in direct proportion to edging ever closer toward new levels of effortlessness in nearly everything we do, barely requiring thought or ingenuity, the more in peril we are of rendering human intelligence superfluous as a first resort to problem-solving. 'Thinking' and 'sensing', as transferred to machines, may, if carried to a logical extreme, ultimately present us with earth-shattering questions, chiefly existential ones. Might not the day come that it is suddenly noticed, to great alarm, that we have inadvertently managed to extinguish any particular need to be alive? Does not a modicum of inconvenience lend character to life, stimulating our mental capacity for problem-solving, for tackling difficulty in a *directly human* way – without which all sense of *purpose* may well be removed from human existence? Are we not in danger of sleepwalking toward extremities at which the object of our endeavours consumes *itself*?

Chapter 5
Social Impact... Has Anyone Noticed?

Much of human conduct, be it motivated by practicality, mischief, lame attempts at edification, personal gain, perceived necessity or any act inciting behavioural by-products ranging from altruism to depravity, of vice and virtue in equal measure, has come to be contingent almost entirely upon the latest technology for its means of execution. And while the computer was rapidly growing indispensable to the success of any competitive business, as the most convenient and efficient means of communication, significant social undercurrents were at play affecting not only the nature of the way information is conveyed but the very conception of its content. In the psychology of consumers, a tectonic shift has taken place over the past quarter century in the fields of information and communication –

without a shred of *conscious* awareness in the public mind. Our perceptions have changed, seamlessly, to the point at which the 'medium' has morphed into the 'message'. Under our very noses! The 'means' by which information is transferred has overtaken the importance of its content, the substance of the very 'message' itself. Emphasis has shifted away from the essence of the 'information' imparted to a fascination with the 'gadget'. The result is that meaning and purpose in communication have been jolted off their original course. Effectively, it doesn't matter *what* you say, as long as you say it through a *computer*, the 'gadget', the only entity that counts, regardless of the gravitas or triviality of that which *is* said. Email me, text me... but don't talk to me.

The social impact of the computer was not altogether unexpected. It was foreseen as a marvel of prodigious and diverse functions from the earliest stages of its evolution, well prior to the advent of the World Wide Web. But the confusion of means with ends in the commercial fields of mass media and communication was a more subtle vision, not as readily anticipated. Nonetheless, by the mid-1960's notable social critics and political commentators were beginning to hint more specifically at the computer's incalculable effects as spotted over the horizon of technological change. The

Canadian academic, Marshall McLuhan, credited with having coined the phrase 'the medium *is* the message' saw it coming a long way off. Half a century later, it's here and it's upon us. By every indication, means and ends, medium and message, have undergone the interchange of importance once foreseen by the shrewder among the pundits. Between then, the decade of the 1960's, and now, research and development in 'microcircuits' by industry in collaboration with academia has made possible the technology of the computer in evermore practical and convenient formats – laptop, iPhone, iPad. It is a bequest not only to modern business practice, but to the whole of society. We all know the narrative.

The fusion of hardware *with* software – of miniscule electronics and its ground-breaking innovation of microchip technology *with* cleverly programmed algorithms – spread over a virtually unlimited network, worldwide, of receiving and dispatch points has produced a fully integrated communications system of unimaginable power and versatility. With the World Wide Web has come the historically unprecedented facility to process information, store it to unlimited capacity in a fashion so organised and contrived as to lend itself perfectly to cross-referencing – search for it, retrieve it on instant demand, disseminate it with astonishing efficiency – and to do it all in a 'centralised' way with a single bit of kit, lightweight and portable at that. The case to be put forth, that, by any objective reckoning, the 'medium' *is* indeed the 'message' is thus made more than compelling. In the intrinsically democratic possibilities it opens up, as a ready means of unrestricted freedom of expression, in the full range and scope of services it can render, this instrument of man is unsurpassed in its manifold effects and implications. But, as with all landmark inventions, it has exceeded its intended outcome.

A new breed of person has evolved. Instantly recognisable as the latest variant of pre-existing social stereotypes, they seem to run on higher-octane energy levels than the rest of humanity. Young, professional and upwardly mobile, their whole existence is subjugated by work and travel. And, though it may do nicely as satirical effect to say that they are in Hong Kong on Monday, Singapore on Tuesday, back in London on Wednesday, only to be off to New York on Thursday – it might also be no more than the slightest of exaggerations. Usually found in the world's major airports or somewhere in the sky at 31,000 feet in a pressurised cabin, their 'office' consists of their laptop, with no fixed location. So intensely in the service of the world economy, they are global not only in the corporate sense, but culturally diluted with no discernible national or ethnic identity.

They are everywhere and nowhere, having no particular need to live in *real time* or *real space*, so advanced is the technology of communication at their immediate disposal. On sacrifice of a leisurely lunch, they prefer to email clients in Beijing, Dubai, Frankfurt; they arrange meetings on Skype with contacts in Chicago, Los Angeles and Tokyo; they 'voicemail' and telephone colleagues in every imaginable corner of the planet from their five-star hotel room – all conducted in the jargon of investment banking, business law, stock market analysis, venture capital and management consultancy. In the breathless pace at which they do nearly everything, the distinction between their professional and private life is barely detectable. With utterly no time or inclination to reflect upon their own existence, the moral worth of what they are doing or their skewed work-life balance, their principal obsession focuses on negotiating the next contract, worrying about performance-related bonuses or the power play of internecine company politics. What sparse social intercourse they have time for, usually at corporate entertainment events or company Christmas parties, is replete with affected – as opposed to spontaneous – vocabulary, overworked phrases, business platitudes, trite anecdotes and banal conversation.

With an attention span of just under two and a quarter seconds for any subject other than money-making, the focus of their life centres on material gain; no other conception of self-enrichment enters their sphere of understanding. It matters not a jot to them what Plato wrote two and a half thousand years ago or what Lincoln said at Gettysburg or that Sibelius incinerated the only existing manuscript of his *Eighth Symphony*. Devoid of any sense of the past, none of these things remotely stirs their interest. As long as their greed is sated by swelling current accounts and medium-term investments remaining secure, the whole of human history prior to the moment of their own biological conception is an irrelevance. Any kind of balanced cross-section of liberal arts subjects, humanities or studies on the historical roots of contemporary civilisation, its fundamental values and moral precepts by which to live – as fields unconcerned with direct money-making or practical entrepreneurship – will have fallen well outside their scope of what's necessary as preparation for life.

Of the two broad varieties of this 'corporate type', the compassionate and the ruthless, the latter predominate as much in the modern age as in the past, and are of greater interest. The former, in the esteemed tradition of Victorian 'do-gooders', endeavour to direct private assets to social welfare concerns and gain in public prestige. The latter are self-absorbed. Single-minded in their pursuit of career success and ruthlessly hard-nosed against anything which threatens it, their sole mission of living on earth is the attainment of personal wealth and power – at any cost. What world view they might entertain, though often cogently expressed, is little more than a self-centred confection of base ingredients: overzealous ambition, inflated ego, unwarranted aggression, brazen arrogance and a sprinkling of like iniquities inhabiting the dimly illuminated recesses of their psyche. Boorishness and insensitivity are their identifying hallmarks; materialism is the deity of their eternal quest. Those of us who have crossed paths with them instantly found cause to wonder if they actually had a soul, or blood in their veins. Yet they leave a resonance; we are prompted to consider larger thoughts, principally those concerning the contradictory nature of man.

Once they have departed our company and are out of sight, questions are left looming. They are such as to remind us, by default, of the rich tapestry of life, the vast range and compass of humanity, its exquisite variety, its dramatic contrasts. How, for instance, can it be possible that the likes of Michelangelo, Shakespeare, Sir Isaac Newton, Beethoven, Harriet Beecher Stowe and Alexander Solzhenitsyn belong to the same species as Hitler and Al Capone? That the chasm between our finest spirits and our most debased can be of such Olympian proportions is a measure of the complexities of human constitution, and a source of endless fascination.

It staggers the imagination that we, as a breed, *Homo sapiens,* have, within current living memory, been responsible for such diametrically disparate phenomena as, say, Auschwitz on the one hand, and socialised medicine on the other. As inhabitants of the globe, we collectively destroyed Europe in a world war, committing heinous crimes against humanity in the process, only to work feverishly in its aftermath to reconstruct – through such as the Marshall Plan – the continent we devastated, setting up for ourselves, while we were at it, a National Health Service, free at the point of delivery. That we are capable of crowning feats of charity, reconciliation, compassion and social justice as well as unmitigated wickedness, both on a scale and to an extent that leaves us bewildered, is an indication that neither modern psychology nor philosophy have yet worked out the internal riddle of man himself. How such antithetical acts can be the work of the same strain of being is not easy to comprehend.

As part of the full range of all that is to be found in nature, the proven extremes of human intrigue are such as to bring into question whether we can trust our own behavioural tendencies, for we have shown ourselves to be as foolhardy as we are wise. Of the generation that bore living witness to the Second World War, irrespective of victor or vanquished – of the magnanimity shown by those who prevailed or the reckoning of retributive justice sustained by the defeated – it can only be said that, collectively, they were participants of world events which brought out the best and the worst in the human spirit. Today's world has its share of fraught and fractious nations, a few of which retain nuclear weapons arsenals of sufficient destructive power to extinguish the whole of humanity. And they are prepared to defend both their ideological and economic interests to no limit. The possibilities for acts of moral redemption, should anything calamitous take place on the world stage, would be far less certain or definable. Can we be at ease in thinking we are reliable, let alone responsible, custodians of Planet Earth?

There can be no better illustration of the tragicomic character of our collective fortunes and exploits than the historical evidence of everything we have crafted and devised in the arts and sciences, in social and economic structures and in our demonstrated concern in seeing their effects come to full fruition as implemented by political agency, private enterprise or state undertaking. From deliberate mechanisms of unimaginable cruelty, instigated as by-products of greed and self-interest, to the loftiest expressions of the human spirit in the arts, literature and humanities, we have *revealed ourselves to ourselves*. As a species, we have composed great symphonies, made life-saving medical advances, graced Europe's elegant cities with magnificent cathedrals dedicated 'to the glory of God', produced Ealing comedies and successfully marketed such concepts as Disneyland. But, in the long purview of our history, we have also committed sustained acts of blatant injustice. We have organised and conducted, over centuries, trade in human slavery as an integral part of the commercial interests of the British Empire and its colonial expansion, arguably the most egregious moral crime *ever*. We have instituted death camps in the Gulags of Siberia, as an instrument of state terror in the design for absolute political control. And, through the poison of indoctrination, persistently and systematically, we see fit to continue committing atrocious acts of mindless terrorism as violent expressions of religious and cultural intolerance. The contrasts are stark and remarkable, but their common denominator is *human* instrumentality. We cannot escape history or disavow our past.

These are all external effects. And despite the obstacle of entire new areas of difficulty, it is sometimes instructive to turn inward, however doubtful the prospect of achieving greater understanding. Human behaviour, as a protean interplay between nature and nurture, has no measurable parameters of either causation or motivation which may help explain it. Psychology is a notoriously imprecise science, even by the new methodologies of its post-Freudian school of 'behaviourism'. All other factors, such as environment, education and social standing being equal, what makes for such character attributes as self-importance? What accounts for altruism? These belong to a category of question on points of human interest which any formal discipline can answer only in part, and even then very tentatively, until the next set of 'latest clinical findings' are published. Even allowing for such as genetic coding or absurdities of oversight like occupying different locations in space, what is it that makes us each different from one another? Why are some of us more appreciative of good fortune than others, grateful for robust health or modest success to the point of making a self-motivated contribution to the common good *in return* for all we have reaped? Yet, how can it be that, at the same time, such a large portion of humanity is unable to fathom the vaguest notion of civic duty or social responsibility beyond so much as begrudgingly paying one's taxes? And, for others still, why is the very thought of public service meaningless unless as an opportunity to exercise prerogative? What is it that makes one person socially well-adjusted, tolerant, open-minded, and the next, self-centred and authoritarian with tyrannical leanings? The world will forever display immense variety in individuals and in nature, but the extreme polarity between vice and virtue and our innate capacity for both is an enigma for which there is no satisfactory explanation. The questions are easy to ask – and almost impossible to answer in terms that could be widely accepted, across all cultures and times. They remain open-ended, as yet to be agreed among diverse academic theories of human personality. At best, we can only make do with idle introspection and perfunctory attempts at making sense of our collective soul. We cannot escape the confines of our own make-up, psychologically, spiritually or culturally.

It may thus be unwise to dismiss our less inspiring examples. They help explain the human condition to its fullest latitude, and ignoring them could be dangerous. As living demonstrations of how we ought *not* to be, they allow us to draw lessons in avoidance, restraint, early recognition of moral obliquity and impending disaster. Taken apart, they are generally little more than one-dimensional philistines with tediously narrow interests, but of value as specimens of study in human turpitude – best observed, though, at a distance.

Chapter 6
Too Early to Tell

Clever technology has also had unintended effects in the simplest, most unexpected of ways, trivial and insignificant on first thought, perhaps not so after some reflection. Few would have foreseen a time when such prosaic items as shelving units in homes and offices might come to be viewed as outdated. In their conventional use for displaying books, any number of communicative formats or decorative items, the utilitarian importance of shelves seems, of late, to have dwindled. Overnight, new technology has made obsolete such and numerous other features of daily life, both aesthetic and functional, heretofore taken as harmlessly everlasting. As a by-product of its inexhaustible capacity to store information *and image*, the computer has affected modern conceptions of both domestic and commercial interior design and decor, of how we outfit a space.

No longer need we clutter rooms with such permanent fixtures as may accommodate our cherished books, DVDs, CDs and LPs. 'Downloading' and 'streaming' have rendered these formats obsolete. 'Cleanline' minimalism is all that's now necessary, bare rooms with everything about anything – you might like to know, read about, look at in either close study or casual perusal, or listen to – tidily stored in your laptop, in software, *not on shelves*. And how are we to display our treasured *objets d'art*, our small artefacts and decorative centrepieces? Where now to place our Ming vase, our marble bust of Beethoven, our gilded fruit bowl, our Meissen porcelain plates and figurines, our priceless Grecian urn? Well, if not on shelves, then, of course, 'online'. Three-dimensional effect on two-dimensional screen has now, since the distant days of 3D cinema, made an unapologetic re-entry into our fresh means of spatial engagement with representations of material reality. Even worse, no longer may we show off our thirty-two volume set of *Encyclopaedia Britannica*, impressing friends with the quality of its binding, the entire corpus, this fount of accumulated wisdom, now vanished into the void, to be drawn up in segments on demand and largely replaced by a citation-deficient 'Wiki relative'. No need to start turning pages when you could just 'click a mouse'. Indeed, entire libraries are now invisible, existing somewhere in cyberspace, the very idea of 'owning a book' radically redefined, elegant neo-classical buildings housing physical publications no longer gracing our urban spaces. It's all changed; and while any characterisation of such change as either good or bad ultimately is entirely subjective, if not altogether too early to determine, that it is irreversible can hardly be doubted. Value judgement as applied to the natural flow of progress is a tricky business when attempted 'close up' – best left, perhaps, to the greater clarity afforded by comparative assessments after the lapse of time.

Yet, these are the internet's least distressing attributions. Truly dangerous vulnerabilities, new, previously undreamt of worlds of concern, have opened up on an international scale, in areas of national security, espionage, cybercrime, identity theft, banking secrecy and data protection. Whether unforeseen, unintended, contrived or desirable, the social, political and commercial consequences are already with us, be they beneficial or otherwise. We even seem to have reached a moment in history at which putting pen to paper is, with growing regularity, judged to be morally questionable, an assault on the reserve rainforests of the vast, but ever-diminishing, Amazon basin, the 'lungs' of our planet, accelerating their imminent depletion. We are encouraged to 'consider the environment' before clicking 'print'. Don't write! Go ecological. When connected to a printer, clicking with haste or abandon is unseemly, unless, possibly, we pause to think of falling trees before so doing; least offensive, putting it all on a 'memory stick' may be the preferred alternative. We have now all become living witnesses to not merely a revolution in information. As the very *psychology* of communication has changed, it is often more thought-provoking, if not elucidating, to ask critical questions of a type formulated as keynotes to argument, than to presume to have answers. Consider the following:

Is necessity *really* the mother of invention, or is it the other way around? Do new technologies give rise to unforeseen consumer demand, to newly procured necessities that weren't there before the invention?

Do we invent something, be it a product or service, and don't quite know what to do with it, feeling at a loss over its commercial possibilities, until we find a way of marketing it? Put another way, in instances where supply precedes demand, do we create markets by manipulating consumer needs through clever advertising and promotion?

Has technology generally improved or diminished the 'quality of life' as opposed to the 'standard of living'?

If judgement is to be passed on the merits of one mode of thought and behaviour over any other, by which frame of reference is it to be done – the former or the latter? Is objectivity at all possible in any such evaluation? On what foundations do we determine criteria for judgements to be made?

Computer geeks are brilliant at pressing buttons but emotionally underdeveloped as fully-rounded human beings. Discuss.

Apropos of 'the application of science to industry' (a widely accepted definition of 'technology') and its commercialisation through manufactured consumer products made easily available, is it possible to devise some means of determining in advance the potential social consequences? And if so, would it be further possible to create conditions favourable to the advancement of those which are of lasting benefit, while avoiding undesirable ones?

If both traditional and contemporary conceptions of behaviour and modes of thought were to be de-contextualised, removed from their time and place in social history, it may, perhaps, be more readily seen that neither is implicitly superior nor inferior to the other. In isolation, they are each qualitatively equal and morally non-committal. Of attitudes and precepts, the new-fangled or modish either altogether fade from the social fringe, or adapt, assimilating into mainstream convention, which, in turn, itself grows to be outdated.

Tradition and modernity are each comparative expressions of time. They are devoid of innate ethical value unless sullied by human meddling – that's to say, if not exploited for self-serving or malicious intentions.

We are all subject to the effects of preconceptions, both our own and those of others, of nurtured affectation, pretension, conceit, posturing – to both good and bad purposes. But, that we can ever escape our own behavioural conditioning is neither desirable nor feasible. As a feature of our natural capacity to adapt to our environment, both public and private behaviour is largely determined by the prevailing social values of time and place, the merits of which can only be relative. Comparisons between old and new ways of governing our lives can never be judged fairly. Context is all. We are products of our time and culture, defined by transient particularities as opposed to dogmatic generalisations. Any close examination of the constituent components of body, mind and spirit that go into a human being's full make-up may well show that we are little more than the contents of our consciousness, the sum total of all our life's experience and past memories, the unavoidable effects of social construct, environment, style of upbringing and all manner of external influence. More generally, 'zeitgeist', the spirit of the age, and all we derive from it, both consciously and subconsciously, shapes us to an extent and in subtle ways we could barely imagine.

Social convention imbues us with a behavioural frame of reference. Yet, departure from its norms, whether inspired or instigated by personal values, bohemianism or any element of counterculture, is, on scrutiny, still identifiable as a tendency of 'conditioned' response to environment, both latent and active, along specific, predetermined lines. Practically the whole of human behaviour, its full range, fits some preconceived pattern that will already have been well studied.

Truly 'authentic' behaviour is scarce. Historically, it is best exemplified by singular lives which, standing above the rest of humanity, 'transcended' all expectation of thought and action. In naming but a few – such as the likes of Dr Martin Luther King, Mahatma Ghandi, Sir Thomas More, Joan of Arc, Jesus of Nazareth, Socrates – we note that martyrdom was their common fate, an all-consuming creed of redemption through sacrifice, their defining precept. But, looking more closely, we come to recognise that their 'being' did not *precede* their 'conviction' – it *accompanied* it. And *that* was the special trait imputing *transcendence* beyond common mores and conventions. Unlike the rest of us, they were living rarities for whom *belief* was integral to, and inseparable from, *existence* itself, their life's example breaching the very limits of moral courage. Needless to say, not many of us are remotely capable of such a grade of virtue or personal resolve.

If anything objective can reasonably be said of this, it is that – apart from the exceptional few – we are, incurably, products of our time *as rooted in the past*, beholden to rules of conduct peculiar to our *culture* and to the *moment* – our beliefs, values and aspirations largely determined by the world into which we are thrust at birth. 'Free will' can, at best, temper and modify these inexorable influences, but never transcend them. The only foundation on which we may define ourselves, now, in the *present*, is that of a psychological landscape as shaped by individual *past* experience. We are 'marinated' in our past to become the *current* product which constitutes both our self-image and the way we are perceived and evaluated by others.

In a sense more disturbing than we might care to admit, we are trapped in our own existence. 'Being' is essentially 'temporal'. We cannot escape time. Locked in the *present*, we are in every way – physical, mental, spiritual – the cumulative effect of our *past*. And though we have only to 'freeze the frame' of time to find we are, at any given moment, nothing more than a living instantiation of *all earlier experience,* the present never stands still. We move with it, ever forward, aging and evolving, as personal development.

Although we are at liberty to think and act, our freedom of choice is restricted, in a deterministic world, by the laws of nature, and, in society, by legal statutes, rules of conduct and the needs of others. We are free to engage our mind to its fullest capacity. Likewise, there is a bewildering range of choices at our disposal regarding how we may behave. But thought and action have limits. And, in a democratic society, the concept of freedom is essentially one of 'negation'. We are limited *internally* by the physiology of human perception and the apparatus for thought and sensation as constituted by our nervous system. We are limited *externally* by Newtonian physics, the material framework of space, time and causality, and by acquired inhibitions imposed by the normative weight of public law and social convention. It is only within these bounds that we are at liberty to exercise free will. And existence itself becomes problematical inasmuch as any conception of freedom is conditional, bound within strict lines of demarcation. It would seem that human aspiration may best be approached through 'authentic' engagement with the world. We must try, in our behaviour, to avoid what Sartre called 'bad faith' (*mauvaise foi)*, vacillation between conflicting mental attitudes within the unity of a single consciousness.

In many of us, *conformity* is often a source of internal conflict against organic tendencies to *deviate from expectation*. Almost all of us are, according to Sartre, in 'bad faith', switching repeatedly back and forth between what he termed *facticity* and *transcendence*, as we go about our daily business.

Chapter 7
Conditioned Consumers

The social, political and economic spheres of life are naturally conflated so as to be inseparable. A vibrant economy is the engine of modern society. And, though recently subject to pressure for change, the prevailing world-economic ethos has been, since the decade of the 1980's, one of *laissez-faire,* free markets and the practical application of 'classical' economic theory as espoused by Adam Smith at the end of the eighteenth century. Business is believed to function at its ideal best when free of obstructive legislation within stable democracies on a global scale. Such a design is thought to tender the best hope in bringing about a 'trickle down' effect, in raising overall living standards, as well as encouraging entrepreneurial initiative, dynamism, diversity and a cosmopolitan perspective in all areas of human activity, as part of an open society. So goes the argument as advanced by the school of free-market economists, habitually presented in idealised form as a theoretical model, but, in its application, nearly always tempered by well-exercised controls: protectionism, monetarism, interest rate adjustment and politically motivated taxation policies. In the current economic climate of Western democracies, though, there is growing doubt regarding the general merits of past practice. Newly emerging world markets and shifts in the wealth-creating centres of gravity among major global economies, coupled with unfavourable outcomes arising from the system's natural dynamic of boom and bust, have, in recent years, initiated a serious rethink.

With deconstruction in the air, alternative economic models in which production and development are reconfigured from the perspective of *social need* appear to be the new creditable thought process. Today, against a world backdrop of rapidly changing political configurations, it is difficult, on balance, to any longer be certain of the wisdom of past prescriptions as viable economic constructs for future wealth creation and the equitable distribution of that wealth. The business culture of deregulation, dating from the boom years of the 1980's, has shown 'trickle down' not to have worked to the penetrative extent it was originally hoped. This now is giving rise to growing concern over the effect of widening wealth inequality on social stability and the future of democracy itself. As an adjusting remedy, the precise manner in which the future of wealth redistribution is formally executed, should this happen, though not entirely predictable, may well rely on fresh ideas as recently articulated by the French economist, Thomas Piketty. In tackling the underlying cause of wealth inequality, to wit, that wealth and capital grow faster than industrial production and output, the suggestion has been put forth that direct progressive taxation of wealth *itself*, as opposed to income, capital gains or gross profit, would tidily eliminate – by means of a structural bypass – all possibility of tax loopholes and avoidance.

Whatever the new adaptation, it is likely to still accommodate free markets, *largely* unencumbered by protectionism, offset by efficient public spending with every imaginable inducement for wealth creation and hopes of ever-improving living standards. And if a new economic model is to be accompanied by any worldwide notion of a democratic way of life, it must also serve the interests of such social dimensions of living as give impetus to civic institutions and for the arts to flourish free of state meddling – all vital to a balanced, healthy and open society. But that, at any rate, is a matter for world governments, and it remains to be seen what new practical economics are instituted over the coming generation. Since the early decades of the twentieth century, mixed economies seem to have produced the desired results with some consistency. In all probability, the future will give us the right mix of carefully chosen elements in the traditions of both Adam Smith and John Maynard Keynes, in which limited state intervention provides stimulus to free enterprise. What is likely to be of greater interest, however, to anyone concerned with the relationship between economics and human behaviour, is the effect of materialism on morality and, more specifically, the subtle influence on the individual of consumerism and retail sales, as visible features of modernity.

There is a case to be made that the *values* directing our purchasing decisions are defined by false conceptions of success, and that, apart from basic necessities, many of our day-to-day purchases are prompted by repetitive patterns of ritualised behaviour as rooted in popular culture. Our shopping habits are nurtured by *synthetic,* not *organic,* needs inasmuch as what we often think to be a *necessity* of life is usually the result of little more than a corruption of certain bourgeois perceptions. In affluent societies, such as our own, we are subject to a range of adverse *effects* arising from well-studied techniques of persuasion as part of the application of consumer psychology by the advertising industry. Such things as self-image, our sense of moderation and of priorities, if we're not careful, can easily be distorted by advertisers in the service of corporate marketing and promotions. Our motivation to buy things does not exist *outside* the machinations of consumerism, but is actually *determined* by them. Moreover, we cannot rightly speak of consumer *values*, unless we have a clear idea of the *method* or *means* by which we can arrive at *criteria* for commercial judgements.

The world ticks on money, trade, commerce. And few better demonstrations of 'medium' as 'message' can be instanced than that of the *representational* value of money as compared to its *intrinsic* value. Though nominally a *means* to an end as a *medium* of exchange – no more than a *transference* mechanism by which human needs or excesses are met and sated through products and services – 'money' is invariably *thought of* as an end in itself. How so? ... Through *greed* ... *avarice* ... that human failing of biblical renown and significance. It is the idea of money as an abstraction that shows how all too effortlessly medium can morph into message. Means become desired ends the moment representational and intrinsic values coincide to assume identical meaning and purpose. *Greed* forces a natural duplicity of mind by which 'money' is simultaneously *both* a 'means' and an 'end'. In theory, money's representational value is *all,* and its intrinsic value practically *nil*. But, our psychology adopts a certain ease of interchangeability. By a greed-driven duality, money, as a medium of exchange, is admitted into the domain of life's permanent commodities and material cravings. How does this happen? In wishing not to exhaust our 'means' too readily, we take a concern in 'stockpiling' it – as *investment*, a kind of 'end' in itself – be it in the form of 'bricks and mortar', share portfolio, ISA, personal pension plan, high-interest current account, 'Blue Period' Picasso, gold bullion ingots or a wine cellar of vintage Chateau Lafite. These, as financial products or saleable items, subject to increase in value over time, are transferable into nothing other than ... money itself ... cash ... exchangeable, in turn, for *the things we want*, the 'ultimate' desired end. However stupendous and wonderful, the human mind is also not without its natural vulnerabilities. 'Money', at various times and in manifold contexts, serves a range of purposes. In so doing, it haunts our ever-changing frame of mind alternately as a permanent fixture *and* as an ephemeral convenience to final intent. In some cases, it does both simultaneously. We make practical use of our homes by living in them, and a few of us might, on occasion, uncork a bottle of Lafite '61 from our cellar. In doing this, we make such direct use of our possessions as to justify an appropriation to them of *intrinsic* worth, as ends in themselves. And indeed, that is what they are. But, as examples, both 'house' and 'wine' are *also* 'money' – because they are marketable 'commodities', having a commercial, or *representational,* value which fluctuates over time, generally increasing. They each are *both* medium *and* message. Giving equal validity to both conceptions, the mind upholds the mercantilist posture of *accumulated assets* in *both* representational and intrinsic form as a direct measure of wealth, while, *at the same time*, supporting the practical view of cash 'in your pocket' or 'in your account' as a convenient *medium of exchange*. Virtually any product or service may be formally commercialised, listed on the stock exchange and ascribed a share value. And ownership of public or private shares in any worthy enterprise would stand as a coveted object of one's efforts and aspirations, often thought of as an end in itself. But, unlike our house or personal stash of vintage wines, the outward manifestation of such ownership, share certificates, *as pieces of paper*, would have little utilitarian or direct use. And while their *intrinsic* worth may be close to nothing, they would assuredly bear a numerically expressed *representational* value as determined by their share price at any given moment of trading on the stock market. That these, and other items of private ownership, are things that *represent* purchasing power as a means to an end is often lost on us. In the mind, they assume *intrinsic* value as ends in themselves and not means; we think of them as commercial *assets* or *commodities*. Yet, they are always representational up to the point at which their market value is *actually transferred*, either in stages or directly, into the *goods and services we want*. 'Money' just plays an intermediary role, only rarely cropping up in the form of cash, almost always making *no tangible appearance at all* except as figures transferred from one bank account to another. That we sometimes hear of share price fluctuations having been affected by 'psychological' factors should come as no mystery. 'Money' has more than one modal existence. At its most *abstract* when expressed as a series of digits in an account, its *physical* forms are endlessly varied: shares, bonds, unit trusts, financial products, freehold properties, cheques, plastic cards and – not to be overlooked as familiar contents of our pockets and wallets – 'hard cash', i.e., minted coins and promissory notes issued by central banks. Our concept of money, 'cut it' as you will, is tinged with greed. And, if we allow it to get the better of us, we see how the very idea of wealth manipulates thought as a prelude to corrupting character – it 'messes with your mind' before it 'brings you down'.

And yet, strangely, it is this greed, this *avarice* – as motivational drive for personal gain and material success –that wakes us up to the realisation that the most elusive of all abstractions universally coveted by man, *happiness,* is more efficaciously pursued *indirectly, as a by-product of self-fulfilment.* Moreover, in the quest for material gain, we also come to see that relationships between people almost invariably bear a complex association to financial success much beyond one's initial thoughts, the interplay of the two emerging as acutely consequential to any sense of personal fulfilment. Ambition may be a common starting point in most self-motivated efforts, but wealth creation as a prerequisite to any productive national economy ultimately feeds on *greed*, one of the seven deadly sins of the Old Testament.

Demonstrably, there are angles of approach by which every human vice can be deployed, if not entirely in a morally commendable way, then in a socially constructive one. If Christian ethics are to be of practical use in mundane existence, then their secular application to any given area of life, from shopping habits to personality clashes, can be of value in *revealing* human character, not just *instructing* it. Underlying individual motive assumes new clarity when scripture is understood as *literature* as opposed to *ritual*. Biblical trope and parable, allegory and metaphor, as components of moral fables for dramatically putting across a point, can be effective sources of daily inspiration, where many a useful maxim may be extracted and applied sensibly to practical living. Examples are part of the mischief of common experience. Do we not, in the ordinary business of daily living, incite our latent flaws and compulsions? And might it not be said we do so nowhere more unavoidably than in many of the shopping habits we develop in which vanity (pride), covetousness (envy) and avarice (greed) wreak havoc with our budgeting limits? Yet, paradoxically, we delight in it, much in the spirit of "Let he who is without sin cast the first stone". Clearly, any one of the deadly sins as mentioned in the Old Testament, *if correctly managed and controlled*, need not be destructive or pernicious. Quite the contrary; it can be socially useful and to the common good. Much of life's experience shows that any of the known biblical transgressions may be actively lived in a 'measured' and moderate way; 'anything goes', if executed in such a manner as to fall within the bounds of public propriety, social convention and established rules of conduct. Have we not been behaving in such an institutionalised way for some two hundred years, since the early stages of the first Industrial Revolution? So in front of our noses that we cannot see it, mass production and free enterprise have allowed us to commodify and market nearly everything imaginable, including underlying motives as driven by biblical sin. The dynamic of sale and purchase, of supply and demand, is propelled by human exigency, desire, indulgence, either synthetic or organic, but nevertheless 'perceived' as necessary, preferable or beneficial. And, as a fillip to any commercial transaction, for both buyer and vendor, these primitive drives are each accompanied by a counterpart to be found among specifically stated biblical vices. Let's consider. Anything held on pledge of 'material gain' (*greed/avarice*), 'personal prestige' (*pride/vanity*), 'instant gratification' (*lust, gluttony, sloth*), 'retributive justice' (*anger/wrath*), 'easy availability' (*gluttony, lust, sloth*), 'one-upmanship' (*envy/covetousness*), 'convenience' (*sloth*), 'status' (*pride/vanity*), 'practicality' (*sloth*), 'modishness' (*pride/vanity, envy/covetousness*), 'appreciation of value over time' (*greed/avarice*), 'visceral contentment' (*gluttony, lust*), 'social advancement' (*envy/covetousness, pride/vanity*), etc., will elicit a 'cash value', a perceived pragmatic worth. It will stake a claim at the marketplace as either a product or service. 'Conditioning' not 'ethics' appears to be the prevailing mechanism by which choices are made in our current, consumerist age. And it would also seem that what we commonly recognise as *acting with financial responsibility* is no different from the behaviour implicit in spending and purchasing, the moral foundations of which are determined by *repetitive patterns of universally accepted practice*. That's to say, doing almost anything that's convenient, suiting individual or corporate purpose, repetitively and at some duration, *without incurring disapprobation* from influential third parties, slowly morphs into 'ordinary', expected or traditional behaviour. It becomes seen as 'right'. Can it not be said that it is here, at the point of purchase and sale, that mild forms of human misdeed may be seen to have assumed utilitarian value? And might it also not be said, with plausibility, that public stock exchanges are barely more than ornate forms of primordial temptation made acceptable under the guise of legal structures of commercialisation?

Such is *how we live,* yet how often do any of us pause to reflect on whether such a state of affairs reduces us by its broader moral implications? It suggests we are not really anchored in abstract principles at all, neither those of religious faith nor of secular philosophy, but rather, by virtue of 'doing' and 'being' – by trial and error – we carve out our own code of ethics as we trudge through life, acting out of little beyond biological instinct. And while a heuristic approach to the 'rights' and 'wrongs' of life may have its merits – inasmuch as learning through practical engagement and self-discovery is known to be an effective cognitive technique – developing the capacity to see through the veneer of appearances into a deeper reality as a starting point for cultivating any sense of moral conscience is another matter. In a world where creating an *impression* supersedes the importance of paying tribute to *truth,* we are ultimately diminished, irrespective of material gain. Notably, throughout various times in the economic history of industrial societies, a sustained rise in the standard of living is often observed to be accompanied, or immediately followed, by moral decline. And though unproven as a formal principle of sociology, can it be that ethics and wealth are inversely related, at least by correlation, if not by direct cause and effect?

As consumers in a media-driven, intensely commercial society, we seem to delude ourselves all too often by failing to make important distinctions between *representational* and *intrinsic* value, *rhetoric* and *substance, image and reality,* the *superficial* and the *profound,* the *meretricious* and the *worthy.* We thus allow ourselves to be susceptible, our emotions tampered with, our hopes exploited, our moral psychology vitiated through consumerism, *as expedited by advertising.* Those of us who love to 'shop till we drop' or find it a source of 'therapy' are living barometers of the lengths we've been driven to, oblivious of our own affected behaviour. We are conditioned to think there's nothing odd about rushing like mad to major department stores during seasonal sales, without pausing to consider the *necessity* to buy as balanced against the idea of being drawn in for no reason other than the limited *availability* of a bargain. Our rationale, almost invariably, that since sooner or later we are going to buy certain products in any event, and it's therefore sensible to do so when they're at a discounted price, is based on a damaging oversight. The more fundamental thought, which often goes unexamined, is *why* we feel the need to make most purchases *at all*. Value for money is never in dispute, but looking more closely at the underlying *motive* for most of the purchases we make is something we have grown disinclined to do, and of which we are barely aware. We live in a commercialised world – we are drowning in it – and having no basis for comparison with any other kind of economic existence, believe rampant consumerism is 'normal'. Surrounded by high-street shops, fast-food chains and gargantuan shopping malls, we cannot readily see the subliminal impact of that which we are in the thick of and are overwhelmed by. Worse, we're seduced by designer labels, beholden to the social pressure sustaining their marketability, and by the sense of false necessity cultivated in consumers by an entire industry devised to promote 'brands' and their associated prestige. In subtle ways, we are made to compete against each other in thinking we mustn't allow ourselves to fall below a certain standard in dress sense and fashion trends. You can't be 'cool' unless you've got *Converse* on your feet, or, for that matter, the handbag simply *must* be *Louis Vuitton*, lest you're refused acceptance into the social circle to which you aspire. Media manipulates our perception of social standing and our interpretation of personal success. It infects our decision-making in ways so subtle as to elude our self-awareness.

Advertisers cleverly know how to exploit not only 'peer pressure', but also what has come to be known as 'status anxiety'. These are but synthetically induced contrivances imposed onto the consumer public by agencies under contract to commercial corporate interests. They are entirely artificial, subjective, implemented with remarkable finesse, making us think we must keep in step with *the latest* – if you will – *modernity*. And if successful retailers know anything at all, they too are adept at how to 'play the public'. How many of us, at the point of sale, will use the phrase, "I think I'll have a 'soft drink'..."? Are we not more inclined to say, "I'll have a *Coke,* or a *Sprite,* or a

Fanta..."? When was the last time we heard anyone say, "I'm flying in an aeroplane"? Is it not vastly more likely they would say, "I'm flying *Easy Jet,* or *Virgin,* or *British Airways*"? Are we not subconsciously programmed to think of the *brand* as the *product?* And does it not suit the purposes of corporate sales that these come to be known chiefly by their commercial name as opposed to a generic description of what the product or service is actually meant to do? Has not the manufactured article, the service or the merchandise morphed, in the mind, into its own instantly recognisable logo or trademark – part of being 'up to date' – making us lose sight of the need they are intended to fulfil as products or services? It all amounts to a forced dissimulation of our sense of priority.

Personal prestige is also played upon. All too readily, do we not think of such products as prescription sunglasses not only as a means by which corrective lenses may filter out harmful rays, but also as an opportunity to flauntingly frame our face with, say, *Dolce & Gabbana*? In the applied psychology of the advertising industry, status and vanity are exploited as convenient catalysts for the manipulation of consumers. A morphing is forced upon us – again, *in the mind* – away from *intrinsic* and toward *representational* value. In the world of designer labels and haute couture, it's not the *utility* that matters; it's the *name*, and its association with lifestyle and status.

Even in the case of mass marketing, 'brand' has overtaken 'substance', presenting 'name' as a direct expression of either aspirational status or fantasy fulfilment. Most people would probably prefer to own a slightly dated *Aston Martin* with a few imperfections in its engine than a latest model, two-seater 'Smart' car that runs perfectly and is easier to park. This is consistent with studies in consumer psychology showing that luxury products are purchased out of a suppressed need to compensate for feelings of inadequacy, self-esteem being outpaced by *perceived* value in the product, which usually is attributable to nothing beyond impressive packaging. *Image* over *substance*: where functionality is expropriated by prestige, we may be assured that our familiar 'friend', rather, our recurring nemesis, *human vanity*, has once again sprung into action.

But an even greater danger is that we develop a taste for 'favourites', for 'brand loyalty', by virtue of the repetitive patterns of our shopping habits. And it is at this point that corporate interests have us 'hooked' – the point at which we, either explicitly or implicitly, express loyalty to a particular brand or label. The very concept of the 'loyalty card' is a manifestation – a symptom not a cause – of a type of consumer addiction as characterised by repetitive behaviour. That I have a certain plastic card in my wallet or am periodically offered discount incentives, I'm psychologically beholden to continue shopping at *Waitrose*, regardless of *Sainsbury's* being more conveniently located. My store account with *Selfridges* ensures, without a second thought, that I walk right past *John Lewis*, where the identical product I might have had in mind is priced marginally cheaper, just to quench the craving for a plastic card 'fix'. I am hooked, incurably, to the point at which being 'never knowingly undersold' pales into insignificance.

The dangers are further compounded with our instinctive reaction of getting similar cards for competitive rival stores, for, in time, the 'snow-ball effect' creeps up – unpayable accumulations of interest charges gradually becoming the material price of a shopping addiction; and so it goes on, ad infinitum. They've 'got us'. And there's the insight. There appears to be no escape from the artificial need to spend money with a certain extravagance. We tend to spend not only beyond basic living necessities, but also in excess of costs incurred over 'necessary' luxury, of what could be morally justifiable in indulging our sense of personal style, taste or refinement, as part of the condition, the very conception, of how we live. It is difficult to see our own folly because it's too close to us, so well integrated into the routine of daily business as to go unnoticed. We think we are 'convinced' of *how to live* in accordance with our personal *likes* and *dislikes,* seldom pausing to consider whether these 'preferences' authentically arise from our own internal grain of temperament and constitution or have been subtly imposed upon us by conditioning influences. All too easily, we fall prey to such commercial enticements as to suppose we are helping ourselves, serving our own interests, by maximising our range of purchasing choices with store cards, loyalty cards, credit cards. But, in truth, we are being lulled into a *false* sense of confidence with deluded notions of buying power and wary consumerism until the wake-up call of debt, the tyranny of unmanageable charges and outstanding balances knock us back into reality.

Generally speaking, we are easily persuaded. Society falls for the 'hype' of commercial advertising, as underpinned by marketing and promotion, no better demonstration of which is the very success of those industries. The 'window dressing' of life plays relentlessly on vanity, that ever-haunting biblical transgression. On many levels, we are attracted to image over substance, conditioned to believe in the merits of what's fashionable, so as not to be 'left out'. This feeds an *acquired* predisposition for *false* necessity and competitiveness within a subtle framework of *conformity* in nearly every aspect of our life. At its most effective, advertising is skilfully crafted to make us 'suspend disbelief'. Sensationalist in its claims and propagandistic in the character of its means, advertising operates through *dramatic* portrayal – within a compressed time frame of, say, a sixty-second broadcast – calculated to penetrate our defences and touch the emotion-sensitive spots of our inner make-up. Human instinct, emotional association and *conditioned* motor response to external stimuli, in which behaviour resulting in pleasure is repeated and anything that might cause pain is avoided, are elements of modern behaviourist schools of psychology, well understood in advertising. These are known techniques of persuasion which advertising agencies apply in precisely targeted ways to incite our dormant fears, unrealistic ambitions and forlorn hopes.

The recruitment of candidates with psychology degrees, in addition to those with formal qualifications in business, is, tellingly, a growing trend in the advertising industry. Not surprising, then, that with characteristic smugness, advertisers will have us believe that driving a certain make and model car will, *in itself*, confer on us the status, if not the living reality, of a successful high-flying entrepreneur. Though fully aware of the extent of their own conceit implicit in the outrageousness of their claims, they also know that all manner of watchdog, consumer-protection advocates and the Advertising Standards Authority will refrain from punitive action as long as formal guidelines are not breached. They know exactly how much they can get away with, often going right up to the edge with great care not to overstep it. Sartre would have been horrified at the extent to which we act on 'facticity' as opposed to 'transcendence', at our gullibility, at the ease by which we allow ourselves to be 'taken for a ride' by commercial interests. And yet, for all their ethical vacuity, such stratagems of economics assist in raising living standards. The contradiction lies within *us, our perceptions* and the *consumer demand* created by ever-*transient* 'values', essentially false ones. There was once a 'cash value' placed on serenading; no longer. We now place enormous worth in wearing the trendiest designer label or having the latest technical innovation in our smartphones and computer software.

Chapter 8
Ages Past ...
Where are we Now?

But how long, it must be asked, before the very notion of the World Wide Web becomes obsolete, even risible? For it surely will in the fullness of time. As Prospero famously proclaims in Shakespeare's *The Tempest*, everything before us is ephemeral, the material world we experience, values and precepts by which we live, convictions we hold as unchangeable certainties, all are "... spirits, and are melted into air, into thin air, and like the baseless fabric of this vision, the cloud-capped towers, the gorgeous palaces, the solemn temples, the great Globe itself, yea, all which it inherit, shall dissolve, and like this insubstantial pageant faded, leave not a rack behind: we are such stuff as dreams are made on, and our little life is rounded with a sleep...". The great Bard further shows us, in *King Lear*, just how tentative and fragile – indeed, dangerous – can be our long-held assumptions and expectations, so easily lent to tragic consequences. Lear's own vanity clouded his judgement when he thought he would command the same level of esteem and authority after relinquishing the burden of power. His life-long trust in the loyalty of his daughters was misplaced, and once stripped of the trappings of state, he was cast into the wilderness to face his irredeemable mistakes. Descending into madness on grasping the full magnitude of what had befallen him, arguably, no other Shakespearean character incites quite the same degree of unmitigated pathos. It is a great tragedy of misjudgement, compounded by sublime self-realisation, a moving insight into human frailty. In some similar fashion – to the extent that great literature is adaptable to dreary, mundane reality – we've all 'been there', on a less exalted scale. We have all made errors of judgement. Most of us have held false preconceptions, suffering their adverse effects when acting on them, learning to bear loss and disappointment. Or we miscalculate and proceed on wrong assumptions, like Lear, allowing vanity and overconfidence to govern our thinking, the bad decision almost always resulting in material sacrifice or attrition of personal morale. But do we ever learn? Only when it hurts, where the stakes are high enough... No wisdom without suffering, no redemption without sacrifice.

In the pre-Christian age of Homeric Greece, a martial spirit, bravado, boastful conceit, 'heroics', imposing one's will by brute force, were esteemed virtues. A millennium and a half later, in an entirely transformed 'Holy Roman' Europe of abiding Christendom, the same qualities marked one out as a prideful sinner. Historical context provides a moral frame of reference to otherwise anodyne human action, our cultural iconography imbued with representational value. Never should it be over-looked that the same Western civilisation that produced Achilles at the gates of Troy also gave us St Francis of Assisi. Be it concrete or abstract, legendary or real, nothing has *meaning* unless it is circumscribed by a *cultural* framework, contextualised by the prevailing values of a *particular* society in time and place. We cannot be said to truly understand an idea, an action or an observable event unless we take into account such things as its related historical and cultural roots of cause, intention and function. Human qualities of merit or acts serving avowedly noble ends and purposes in one context can, in another, be a source of hubris – foredoomed by nemesis, followed by rapid downfall. All is 'comparative', and the case for moral 'absolutes' rests on shifting ground. It's not bare, unadorned 'facts' that import meaning, it's their 'evaluation' in the light of time, place and circumstance, without full knowledge of which judgement can never be objective.

On serious debates of life, it's often said there is an implicit arrogance and humbug in claims of taking the 'moral high ground'. The reason lies no further than the absence of *objective* standards for universally applicable codes of ethics. There are formal branches of philosophy – notably, modern existentialism – which argue there is no moral foundation to the world whatsoever; we are, instead, presented with a random, anarchic and bewildering array of choices in a godless universe. And though the welter of operable decisions this allows us is clearly a triumph of free will over predestination, we exist to no ultimate purpose. Other schools of thought present the starting point for the metaphysics of morality as a particular conception of evolutionary survival of the fittest, Darwinian natural selection, a biological struggle for life and death between nature's prey and predator – defining an ethic that goes beyond good and evil. It is a fundamentally dark and pessimistic view of the world and of human existence, a frightening region to tread, though much has been studied and said of it.

We function within a *particular* culture as determined by *time* and *place,* and are subject to the influence of its standards and prescribed expectations. Though agents capable of exercising free will, we are beholden to laws and conventions of that society, and, more broadly, to its adherent *values*. Each epoch leaves a legacy peculiar to itself. We, today, are not citizens of the city state of Athens in the fifth century BC, nor are we humanist figures of High Renaissance Europe. And though *distantly* rooted in these periods, our *immediate* legacy comprises the political, social and economic order of the democratic nation states of Western Europe in the wake of the Second World War. Our claim to enlightenment derives from our tradition of liberal political theory, dating from late eighteenth-century conceptions of liberty, equality and democracy. And we ever aspire to social progress, economic betterment and a secure future, continually seeking, through democratic processes of debate, the fairest and most efficient means of achieving these. Everything is of its time, place and circumstance. Human conduct is largely motivated by *particularities,* and moral judgement based on universal standards often ill-applies to specific cases.

If we are to be judged, it cannot be *solely* in terms of advanced science and technology, or even a commonly shared code of ethics. Civilisations are also assessed by their art and literature, architecture, standards of literacy and education, political and civic institutions, the legal system, the 'social contract' between government and citizen – whether codified in law or implied by tradition

– conceptions of state authority as balanced against individual liberty, quality of life, industrial development, the capacity for wealth creation, social mobility, standards of medical treatment, life expectancy and by their *faith,* both religious and secular, *as applied to social ends.* These are all vague 'indicators', in the absence of features of life and society that are measurable with any degree of precision. But they provide some sense of the character, ambitions, level of enlightenment, public concerns and private pursuits of a given civilisation within the continuum of time and place. Although not formally quantifiable, there is still much that can be made legible from simple observation of *the way we live* and the cultural framework within which we do so.

It would seem that much of private behaviour is governed by pressing choices to be made, not necessarily between what is commonly perceived as 'right' or 'wrong', but, rather, by an instinctive sense of 'the best play' to be made in a difficult situation. Like all abstractions, 'virtue' is not *objectively* measurable as a parameter of value judgement or any universal code of morality. By being practical, in doing 'whatever works' to suit our own purpose, we often act without *conscious* reference to formal rules of conduct or to the needs of others. In a Machiavellian world, we are innately self-centred creatures, survival instinct ultimately reverting us to type. But this is largely concealed by civilisation itself, which tempers any savage or destructive proclivity with guiding obligations – by providing *structures:* laws, conventions, traditions – whereby individual conduct, *in aggregate,* produces a degree of collective benefit and social improvement, the mechanism of Adam Smith's "invisible hand". The cumulative effect of our lone pursuit of self-interest is to the advantage of society as a whole.

Effectively, we are all reduced to simply doing whatever we *can,* and, with surprising frequency, it is to considerable achievement. In her international success as an operatic soprano, Maria Callas was notable as having had flawless technique and consummate musicianship. But it was not those features of her talent that distinguished her or made her what she was; it was her capacity to convey the full emotional impact of an aria within the context of the opera's wider dramatic narrative. She was able to do so in a uniquely intense style, reducing audiences to tears, winning a loyal fan base and to great critical acclaim. Her dynamic range coupled with the particular timbre of her voice, and the pathos it invoked, connected with an appreciative public in a distinctive and incomparable way, special among fellow singers of her generation. It was a case of 'content', not 'form'. It was 'the best play' delivered along the fringes of formal structure. Skill, craft and technical perfection are commendable – but spontaneous, targeted emotion cannot be taught. What this tells us is that success comes from different directions and is related to modernity through comparing, often with delight, the past, present and future. It tells us that the traditional or anticipated way of doing things is but one among many in achieving our desired ends – 'form' being subservient to 'content' – providing us with instructive examples in which features of modernity may be observed to deliver the designs and aspirations of unchanging human pursuits in surprising ways.

The great Finnish composer, Jean Sibelius (1865 – 1957), saw fit to burn the only existing manuscript of his *Eighth Symphony*, feeling unable to complete the work as *he* would have liked. Hardly a matter of 'right' or 'wrong', he was consumed by self-doubt over the growing influence of modernist trends in musical composition. After years of anguish in trying to perfect it, destroying his own creation addressed the need for vindication of honour, demonstrative of an inner law of personal conviction by which frustration of will morphs into moral rectitude. He made 'the best play' in an impossible struggle between the demands of public expectation and a conscientious commitment to the integrity of his art. His *Symphony No. 7* – successfully completed, published, recorded and now occasionally performed – was premiered to a grateful world in 1924. It was 'structurally' innovative as symphonic content in a single movement. His 'stillborn' *Eighth* was to have been entirely radical in 'content' with unconventional departures from traditional harmonic progressions and tonal areas. But Sibelius could not entirely convince *himself* that what he was doing was art and not artifice. As a 'fourth-generation' composer of the Romantic Period, now finding himself in the early decades of the twentieth century surrounded by a new musical climate of 'atonality', 'neoclassicism' and serious reassessment of the foundations of traditional harmonic theory, the very 'grammar' of musical composition, modernity – the modernity of *his* age – had got the better of him. Apart from the well-received tone poem *Tapiola* (1926), he composed nothing of significance after the *Seventh Symphony* (1924) during the remaining thirty-three years of his life.

Humanity, by and large, finds ways to live with the lasting effects of radical upheaval, adversity and hardship, on both an individual and a broader societal level. As a species, we are adaptable in extraordinary and unexpected ways. The resilient texture of 'everyday life' survives wars, plagues, earthquakes, epidemics, famines, as well as internal personal anguish, no matter how severe or prolonged. When the catastrophe is over, people 'get on with it', adapting to its long-term imprint, learning to live with every repercussion of change. From any historic disaster that could be named – the Black Death of 1348, the Great Fire of 1666, the London Blitz of 1940 – we have recovered, bounced back and plodded on. And as generations come and go, it's precisely this unflagging resilience that ensures fertile ground for *ever-new* modernity to flourish.

Chapter 9
Old as New, New as Old ... Memory and Nostalgia

Yet, 'modernity' as a subject, and what we *think* we mean by it, may not be at all easy to grasp when scrutinised. Any coherent or general definition is hard to come by. If confronted with the direct question, "What is 'modernity'?", we are likely to note that it is far easier to recognise examples of modernity than it is to formally define the term itself. It has little substance beyond vague claims that it is everything within our range of perception which has *only recently* grown to be acceptable among new behaviours and practices, forming a definable pattern, as driven by new attitudes of mind. We may plausibly say it is a natural condition of the present – as constituted *at any given moment in history* – initiated by the latest generation in reaction against anything perceived as antiquated.

But it eludes rigorous description or interpretation that can be understood worldwide, by all cultures and throughout time. We can, with reason, identify it as anything not outdated; we may say it is anything in current fashion; we can spot it in certain elements of living patterns of the present. We know, imprecisely, what is associated with it: new ways of doing things arising from new technologies, commercial innovation, social upheaval or fresh trends in couture, hairstyle, car design, architecture, interior decor, cuisine – that is, any conspicuous change recently incorporated into our accustomed way of living. Modernity keeps moving. It is 'time-dependent'. There is *the* modernity of today, and there are the *many* 'modernities' of times past. There was a time when indoor plumbing and household electrical power were features of modernity – no longer.

If asked, "What does modernity *look like?* How do I know it when I see it?", we might reasonably reply that, as *currently* constituted, it ranges from pure abstraction, as an attitude of mind or peculiarity of demeanour, to such concrete manifestations as, say, a fully equipped domestic kitchen fitted out with every imaginable state-of-the-art household appliance. It may also consist of the latest and most advanced medical technology for laser ablation of cancer cells. In all their variety, visible examples are not difficult to spot. But less tangible instances of modernity's multifaceted appearance are often noted in speech and physical bearing. It is to be seen and heard in esoteric uses of spoken language, newly-forged expressions, unestablished idioms and non-standard vocabulary, the latest street slang or certain turns of phrase as practised by some among the latest generation, often accompanied by corresponding hand gestures and body language. When anything offbeat is accepted, widely copied and done repeatedly, it tends to become 'manneristic' – a term now generally applied to forms of addictive behaviour but derived from a specific period, pre-baroque, in the history of art, characterised by contorted figures. We see it today in a growing tendency to use a rising intonation in the cadences of common speech by which *every* verbal utterance is unintentionally presented as a rhetorical question. Manneristic, indeed! We often see it in non-verbal fashion statements, as in, say, body art, pierced flesh or a pair of jeans horizontally slashed at the knees. These are all current instances of 'modishness' *as part of* a wider 'modernity'.

And in each case, value judgement of any sort would be misplaced without recognition of the need for contextual distinctions. Much of what we see on the surface of things is *contingent* as opposed to *intrinsic*. Torn clothing, as an example, if not 'time and place specific' or accompanied by affectations of modishness, may just as well be taken as 'poverty', not a conscious expression of 'fashion' – a case in which the same visual effect, subject to multiple interpretations, would emphatically not constitute an instance of modernity – for poverty is independent of time, where fashion is not. Evaluation, interpretation, meaning are all variables in our direct perception of sense data, entirely dependent upon time, place, mental approach and underlying cause or intention, usually deliberate, occasionally unavoidable. In validating genuine instances of modernity, we can have no reasonable grounds in assuming that torn clothing is necessarily a symptom of either fashion *or* poverty; equally admissible is such human caprice as sheer neglect, indifference or a tribute paid to retro-1970's 'punk'. Lacking in originality, these are far from authentic fashion statements. They are symptoms of either 'countercultural conformity', derivative of an outdated craze, or desultory acts made on a whim, 'context-free', as one-off expressions of personal style with little or no grounding in the past or present. The range is as inexhaustible as all that lies latent in the human psyche.

The context of time and place, of popular culture, of circumstance and attitude, ascribes 'value' – that is, how we are predisposed to comprehend a particular social phenomenon. We appropriate meaning to what we see and hear by what is *internal to us,* as observers. And our preconceptions change as *time* – the catalyst by which modernity morphs into convention – then tradition, impels public perceptions to adapt to changes in the external world. There will always be an '*avant-garde*' in the arts, a 'state of the art' in technology and an 'all the rage' in fashion. Modernity is *time-dependent*. It is always *of a period*. And it is *transient*, never standing still. Young men sporting long hair in the late 1960's and early 1970's was perfectly in order as social convention – but *only* after the initial outrage over it had dissipated. The same general phenomenon – that of unorthodox or outlandish appearance – a generation prior, in the 1920's and '30's, may have had different connotations: bohemianism, eccentricity. But it was socially acceptable as an approved expression of anti-authoritarianism. Both cases were deliberate statements of personal preference, but they were each observable examples of modernity originating from different areas of life. One was part of what had evolved out of the 'rock scene' into mass popular culture as the 'beat' generation was morphing into the 'hippie' movement, the other came out of modernist aesthetic trends which characterised a specific part of the early twentieth century. But the feature they share as manifestations of modernity, each *of its own time*, is the contrast with their *immediate* past and the sense of peculiarity, marvel or antipathy incited in the *early* stage of their social origin. These, as examples of modernity, are qualitatively different from, say, general belief or ideology, such as political affiliation or religious commitment – sentiments which stand outside the specificity of time and social context.

Principles, convictions and faith, when genuinely held, are universal and eternal in character, not dependent *for their existence, essential meaning or value* on time and place; they cut through the timeline of all period 'modernities', which, by contrast, are particular and *brief* in their examples and representations. Being, say, 'progressive', 'liberal-minded' or politically 'left-wing' is not, in itself, being 'modern', for these are elements and characteristics transcendent of time. It has been said that such political ideologies as communism and socialism are manifestations of current modernity. But if, by definition, modernity is to be 'time-dependent', we've only to look at Plato's *Republic* to be disabused of the suggestion that there's anything new in such a conviction. We note that over two millennia ago, a political theory was advanced in support of the idea that in an ideal polity the objective interests of the individual citizen are engineered to coincide with those of the state, but that ultimate success in such a model is for the benefit of the state, *not* the individual. Can anything be more Marxist in spirit? Being on the 'left' of the political spectrum is not, *of itself*, 'modern' – it's timeless. And if ever it *was* 'modern' as an idea, it hasn't been so for over two thousand years. By way of contrast, 'modern-*ism*', as an early twentieth-century aesthetic movement, though not a *current* example of 'modern-*ity*' – for we are now in the world of post-modernism – is an example of a *past* modernity. As a matter of semantics, 'modernist' trends constituted examples of 'modernity' *in their day,* and provide a useful illustration of modernity as a time-dependent concept.

By these parameters, anything independent of time, place or intention, and not contingent on a predisposed mental attitude, cannot stand as modernity. At any random moment in history, that which is new is discernible as that which is salient, standing out against the general backdrop of long-established conventions and standards in every field of human activity – the arts and humanities, the sciences, business and commerce, popular culture – and established patterns of *how we live*, defined lifestyles. But *current* modernity, all that hasn't appeared until the latest generation, is an integral part of the whole of contemporary life, the now – *which includes the involuntary memory of all past modernities.* The present – *any* given *present* in time – apart from nurturing its own contemporaneous modernity, also carries with it all accumulated past modernities, be they conceptual, in the mind, or tangible, as physical objects.

Once described as 'dregs of society', many an aging rock star, having enjoyed what many thought dangerously subversive early success in the heady days of the 1960's, is today an inconspicuous part of 'the system', an icon of the music industry. Socially, culturally and technologically, the instance, on each level, is not difficult to comprehend as part of a larger phenomenon. From early beginnings at the cutting edge of life, as either a welcome new source of mass appreciation or a strange curiosity of bourgeois disapproval, or envy, alike, to full integration as a part of the fabric of current popular culture and the *nostalgia* of 'now', the journey of an ephemeral 'modernity' can be seen in so much of today's popular imagery and symbolic meaning. Hollywood, the rock scene of the 'swinging sixties', supersonic aviation, ocean-going luxury, as arbitrary examples providing fertile ground for illustration, have their origins in the past but are also part of current iconography. Such disparate phenomena as, say, Fred Astaire dance musicals, The Rolling Stones, Concorde or sailing across the Atlantic on the Queen Mary are all indelibly imprinted in our collective consciousness as images and activities apprehended either vicariously, through mass media or by direct experience. Once on the innovative fringes of a particular past as active modernities, they now remain with us forever as 'cultural memory', ordinary features of the present.

Though still a public celebrity, Sir Mick Jagger is today an establishment figure whose *original* fame is squarely of another time, the 1960's. The Queen Mary is now a museum open to the public, in permanent mooring and a source of envy to visitors who are dazzled by the ocean-going luxury of its heyday, the 1930's. Concorde, very much of the 1970's, is now seen as a precarious venture, financially unviable and technologically premature, but still enduring as a *memory* of dashed hopes in commercial supersonic aviation. And as for Fred Astaire, an eternal fixture of American show-business talent and success, few images of popular entertainment or portrayals of style and elegance as devised by Hollywood studios in the Depression-addled world of the 1930's can be better conferred to the mind. For many, and quite rightly, watching Fred Astaire dance on the silver screen is simply one of the great delights of life. All were of the past, but still remain with us in iconic form *in the mind*. It would seem that when the modernity of a specific period fades with the passage of time, its imagery stays behind – forever. We are left with a collective matrix of impressions, an 'archaeology' of popular and high culture, without which the marketability of such items as antiques and 'nostalgia' – antiquarian books, prints, maps, periodicals, photographs – period-style building design or interior furnishing, vintage products of industrial production, such as steam engines and old 'classic model' cars, would be untenable. That such things remain commercially viable as practical realities serving current tastes and delectations is testament to the idea that the present is inclusive of all elements of the past; times may change and 'all is flux', but *collective memory* is inextinguishable.

The phenomenon of 'social stereotypes' is a curious case of hybrid modernity – that's to say, one with the *structure* of timeless continuity, but not the *substance*. It is to be seen all around us, yet easy to miss for all its prevalence and familiarity. As urban dwellers in a densely populated environment, we develop, in our thoughts, a 'composite' profile of commonly observed 'types', societal groups of a certain commonality, comprising persons we tend to place in ill-defined categories: the Islington 'Literati', the Camden Town 'Hipsters', the Chelsea 'Celebrity Set', the 'Trendies' and 'Financiers' of Notting Hill, the City Road 'Dotcom Entrepreneurs', the 'Creative & Media' Moguls of Hampstead and St John's Wood, the 'Oligarchs and Zillionaires' of Knightsbridge and Belgravia, the 'Dandies and Fashionistas' of Saville Row and Jermyn Street, the 'Art Dealers and Connoisseurs' of Bond Street and St James's, the 'Socialites' of Cheyne Walk and Cadogan Square, the 'Artists' of Shoreditch, the liberal 'Arrivistes' of Primrose Hill, the 'Cineastes and Bohemians' of Soho, the 'Young, Upwardly Mobile Professionals' spread all over the place, with high concentrations in Battersea, Islington and recently gentrified pockets of the East End, the 'Civil Service Bureaucrats', the 'City Bankers', and, of course, those close relatives of the Chelsea Set, the legendary 'Sloane Rangers'.

These are all 'London-centric' images hatched in the mind, made up of features configured in such a way as to determine a general social identity: career, location, dress sense, personal presentation, tech-savvy confidence, topically informed conversation, well-connected circles, professional slickness, financial solvency and involvement in some aspect of wealth-creative innovation in their field of endeavour. As descriptive of modernity, these nominal elements are of a 'time' and 'mental attitude'. Yet, the larger superstructures to which they belong, the *non-modernities*, are everlasting; changing demographics and shifts in social trends are an inevitability over time. But, intriguingly, what makes stereotypes objects of such interest is the fact that they do not truly exist outside the mind. We have subconsciously conjured them up on the basis of some limited reality. As paradigms of the imagination, they provide us with a source of reassurance that we may have to hand some understandable frame of reference that squares with our social preconceptions. At best, they are generalisations descriptive of the 'ideal', not the 'real', nothing more than a synthesis in our heads, used occasionally to disarm ourselves of any suppressed need for parody.

Cross-influences and a diversity of interests are prominent in vibrant metropolitan cultures. And living examples of social stereotyping which might be a subject of study will likely contain elements of several categories. It's perfectly possible I could be a high-profile television, stage and screen personality, yet live nowhere near the King's Road, Chelsea – or Hampstead or Highgate for that matter – but instead in, say, Islington, with left-leaning intellectuals as next-door neighbours or in Cheyne Walk among faded rock stars and City bankers. The mixture of ingredients bucks the idealised model, but gives the living reality its essential character. Was the world ever any different?

We create non-existent generalisations from an endless riot of particulars. And, while all attempts at 'profiling' are bound to contain impurities, the common element is *transience:* our examples are selective in meeting specific preconditions. For, to state the obvious, there exist social stereotypes which do not constitute examples of modernity and, conversely, there are modernities which are not social stereotypes. For this reason, exclusion is unavoidable for such as, say, Welsh sheep farmers or Oxford academics, being stereotypes but not modernities; they are static, not time-dependent, outside metropolitan scenes of frantic living which provide impetus for rapid change – the defining difference between the city slicker or bourgeois suburbanite and the country squire.

Abstract ideas may originate almost anywhere, as likely on farms as in oak-panelled dens or the laboratories of effete academia. But, before any change is initiated – the metamorphosis delivering an idea to its completed state, from starting point as a mind's abstraction to practical application as a commercial product available to consumers at a retail price – such ideas necessarily undergo gruelling and rigorous intermediary stages. They are subjected to exhaustive testing by research and development divisions of global companies, often working in collaboration with universities and academic institutions. They are scrutinised and monitored by government regulatory agencies, ensuring legal compliance. They are brainstormed by think tanks, as sources of information to government quangos. They are wrested by marketing departments as prototype models for feasibility studies. Thoughts on 'the thought' – an evaluation of the original idea – will be expressed, put about, exchanged, embroidered by these interacting concerns, all focused on a solitary binding argument: some convincing justification for the idea's ultimate success at the marketplace. And, though academic institutions are a staple as venues for research projects in engineering and technology as well as the natural and social sciences, it is through industry alone that the end result is made possible. At each stage, by which the abstraction morphs into the viable commercial product, formal efforts are made to protect it by corporate legal departments. Any new, exciting, cutting-edge innovation is appropriated in law as 'intellectual property', patented, copyrighted, branded and marketed before being retailed and finally deployed by the public. This final *material* version, the saleable item as the completed state of an original idea – targeted at a consumer public – is showcased in cities, in industrial centres and enclaves of high-tech innovation. Towns first developed out of trading posts, centralised points of commercial transaction. It is no accident today that global stock exchanges are located in *financial* capitals: New York, London, Paris, Frankfurt, Hong

Kong, Tokyo, etc. The genesis of ideas may take place in virtually any human context of time and location, but in their passage into social and commercial use on a worldwide scale, they, at some stage between thought and material reality, are bound to be subjects of discussion in corporate boardrooms – headquartered, almost exclusively, in, or on the outskirts of, big cities. The dynamic of transience would otherwise not apply and no element of modernity could consequently be highlighted or studied.

Change is natural, and it's a fair thought to say that demographic change is almost always the end result of commercial endeavour. At the same time, the substructure under which the thought is framed contains features of permanence, for, historically, there have always been concentrations of particular socio-economic classes from one district to the next throughout the industrial world's major cities. And they have always evolved and transformed through the dynamic of demographic change – urban renewal and capital investment, emigration and immigration, and public redevelopment by joint venture between local authority and private trusts. The element of modernity lies squarely in the mutations brought about by the mainspring and fluidity of demographics, with either gentrification as the outcome of new sources of local wealth creation, or faded charm giving way to decay and dereliction as a result of neglect, yet with the prospect of opportunities to be exploited by property developers, spawning revived hopes of regeneration. The specific make-up of concentrated population flows *is* time-dependent, but the occurrence of the general phenomenon of inevitable shifts in urban population is timeless. As a defining distinction to be made, social stereotypes are an example of modernity in 'content', but *not* in 'form'. An interesting inversion of this may also be demonstrated through our collective awareness of 'historical' stereotypes, emerging from fiction, legend, recorded chronicle, primary and secondary sources of all descriptions. By virtue of the vibrant media culture in which we live and the incalculable influence it has exerted on us, mainly subconsciously, there are certain imprinted features of a cognitive tableau, a pageantry of the mind, we cannot dispel. We all have some animated conception of, say, 'Dickensian characters', 'Regency dandies', 'Southern belles', 'Prussian officers', 'Mexican banditos', 'mad kings', 'French revolutionaries', 'Caribbean pirates', 'Georgian gluttons', 'Restoration libertines', 'Elizabethan courtiers', 'monastic monks', 'medieval crusaders' or 'Roman gladiators'. Where on earth does it all come from? Far from being a feat of pure imagination, it is an exploit of 'conditioning';

be it Hollywood, world cinema, television, original literary classics or the internet, we have drawn mental impressions from unavoidable sources of mass media all around us, the lasting imagery of which, whether of the present or of a fancifully reconstructed past, cannot but remain in our communal store of cross-cultural references. In this, the essential elements of modernity are to be found in the 'form' – the process, the 'contraption', the medium, the agent, the means, the 'gadget', the intermediary – *not* in the 'content', not in the image itself. Nothing of substance can be conjured up or evoked without the technical means of retrieving and presenting it. And, where social stereotypes are a case of content over form and ends over means, historical stereotypes are its transposition: means supersede ends and form precedes content.

Throughout the history of commercial cinema, the content of film narrative generally consists of either original storylines or dramatic reconstructions of past events. But a motion picture made in, say, 1935 will inevitably have a different feel and look about it from one on the same subject and theme produced at some future date, three or four decades later. Change in the *technology* of film-making and innovation in nearly every aspect of cinema during the intervening years will have made an old story look new when presented as a 'latest' version. Cinematography will be more advanced in its hardware and more contemporary in its techniques of application. Studio production values will almost certainly have changed. The screenplay will, in each instance, be written with updated dialogue to reflect prevailing social values of the day, shifts of language use, or newly discovered twists and points of reference in the historical backdrop of the narrative. Different schools and traditions of acting will be evident among the cast in each of the different productions. The montage editing and cross-cutting, the sequence in which successive shots are ordered and juxtaposed to convey a deliberate meaning to the unfolding narrative, will comply with the creative fads of the day. And the directors, as *auteurs* of the project, will each have a different conception of the plot and its points of emphasis. It's the same story made fresh *by virtue of new means of conveyance* within the context of a modern outlook. Yet, as products of mass entertainment, 'remakes' seldom seem to have the commercial success of the original, nor the critical acclaim. As an example, we need look no further than the MGM productions of *Mutiny on the Bounty*. The original (1935) starred Clark Gable as Fletcher Christian opposite Charles Laughton's Captain Bligh. Precisely twenty-seven years later, the 1962 release gave us Marlon Brando and Trevor Howard in the respective roles. After a similar span of time, the latest version, a co-production, cast Mel Gibson with Anthony Hopkins, giving us contrasting styles of acting, new sensations off the screen, different reaction among the viewing public, fresh emotional emphasis in the narrative and varied critical response – all because society is in a constant state of flux. What does this tell us of modernity? That it is a 'dynamic', a 'means', a 'process'. It 'repackages' old, well-known content, presenting it anew. The human need it addresses is eternal, the means of addressing it, ever changing.

The significance of this is paramount, as yet again we see how the medium morphs into the message, not in the sense of 'interchangeability', but in that one is a necessary outgrowth of the other, the two inveterately linked as cause and effect: there can be no image without its mechanism for projection, no substance outside its structural framework, no goods without a means of delivery. The technology of modern life makes the whole of the past accessible, intelligible. It allows us, through our efforts at achieving accurate and faithful dramatic reconstructions, to establish spiritual links, to commune with different times and places. If we equip ourselves with the requisite enquiring methodology – one that seeks to develop some understanding of the underlying influences by which people thought and felt as forged by 'the spirit of the age' of a chosen historical epoch -- the past can become surprisingly relevant. And if we're to any extent imaginative, we would do well to be *selective* of those features of the past which best adapt to the practical needs and realities of the present. We'd be altogether unwise not to draw from our prodigious wealth of heritage. But without the past, there would be nothing to engage with. And without the technology of the present, the vividness of the past could never be brought to life. Past, present and future, as divisions of the abstraction of 'time', are part of a single unity of 'being'. That existence, ideas and how they are interrelated are inescapably temporal is seen by the impossibility of separating ourselves from the ineluctable structure of time, space and causality. These are built into the fabric of our capacity for conscious perception of the world.

In proclaiming "the *medium* is the *message*", Marshall McLuhan was levelling a profound argument. 'Content' is affected by the very 'means' of its conveyance in a way that determines the emotional impact or desired effect it has on the spectator, listener or observer. How many of us have emerged from a theatre, back onto a public pavement – having just watched a film with a *powerfully delivered* message – still in a state of half-mesmerised suspension of disbelief? It takes us a few minutes, at least, to 'snap back to reality'. The *medium* of cinema did this to us, not the story per se, but the way the story was crafted through the art of film by a skilled and talented director. It was the effectiveness of the delivery, the means – not the content. Truly, medium as message! Film, perhaps to a greater extent than all other media, has the power to lower the mental faculties, to shift our focus of consciousness away from our immediate physical surroundings and transport us to an emotional realm of another time and place.

And it is in this understanding of the nature of cinema that we may best see the effectiveness of the message being intimately bound to the medium. Within each frame, there is a certain composition of visual cues, be it in close-up, medium or long shot. Each stretch of related frames carries dramatic content, and when edited into a 'montage' sequence, in which a series of shots are deliberately juxtaposed in compressed time to convey meaning and propel forward the narrative, we find cinema exploiting its most natural inherent property, the capacity to manipulate the space-time continuum. In addition to this, we have the camera's facility for 'tracking', 'panning', zooming in and out, along with the further trickeries of the cutting room: 'fading', dissolving', split-screening, jump cutting, parallel editing, superimposing, computer graphics imaging and all manner of special effects. These technical elements comprise the intricate clockwork that is cinema. And when the complementary dimension of sound – speech and music (both 'commentative' and 'actual') – 'warms up' the screen, bringing the whole to life, we have what McLuhan refers to as a 'hot' medium: whereby the spectator need make no effort of their own to be affected by the full force of the communicative format before them. It is not surprising that film has been said to be the ideal instrument of propaganda. As an effective means of persuasion, it is unsurpassed in its efficacy to penetrate the veneer of awareness and touch the subconscious mind. No art form, at its most affirmative and eloquent, can more thoroughly captivate, enthral or render us to a dream-like state. Film... quite possibly the ideal, the purest, example of medium as message.

In different guises and ever-new transformations, modernity has always been with us; there can be no present without the past. It is but a function of time, part of any randomly chosen moment, an illusory present, receding perpetually into the past as a snap expression of cultural evolution over millennia. Elements of today's modernity will at some future time constitute 'quaint relics of history'. Imperceptibly, 'today' morphs into *both* 'yesterday' *and* 'tomorrow', the former entirely in the mind, as memory, the latter, in the dynamic of a fleeting present ever advancing forward. What is modernity if not but fragmentary features, both material and conceptual, of 'now', and what is 'now' if not the future's past? With no formal definition being entirely adequate or satisfactory, 'modernity' might best be *thought of* as the re-adaptation of 'means to an end', of reusable old ideas being passed on from one generation to the next, rules of custom serving eternal human needs, the *updated* form of which is actuated through the latest technology or commercial expediency but still tending to the necessity of unchanging function. As such, we ought, more rightly, to be focused on 'civilisation' when speaking of 'modernity', and how permanent necessities are met in new and different ways throughout time. There can be no such thing as being 'modern' or 'fashionable' or availing ourselves of technology's latest trappings unless we bother to define such notions in specific terms, as peculiarities of a moment in social evolution. Can it be that its very elusiveness as a concept to be truly understood gives evermore credence to the suggestion that modernity – however we choose to define it – is indeed non-existent, and that we are forever deluding ourselves in thinking there is anything new under the sun?

Chapter 10
The *Best Play* – We're all at it

When people used to wear reparable shoes, handwrite on paper or be inclined to break into spontaneous song, it almost seems to have been a different world. Was it *really*? Is it not the very simplicity, the artlessness of the impromptu act, especially with song, that constitutes the most natural expression of the human spirit? Are we now fundamentally any different than in the past? Surely not. Are we any better or worse off than at any time in the past? Materially and technologically, far better – undeniably so – for we have extended life expectancy, raised living standards beyond all recognition and increased the efficiency of nearly everything we do.

But the question is unanswerable where morals and manners are concerned. As functions of time and culture, 'relative' values and ethical 'ambiguity' seem to be the normal state of human affairs, the default condition of a world which is eternally grey, never black and white. There is no definitive interpretation of the world or of existence. Human evaluation is unavoidably self-referenced. There are those who take a coldly rational, sterile view of life. Others tend to see things in a sentimental light. And there is a significant portion of humanity inclined toward an aesthetic appraisal of nearly everything around them. The social and political satirists' view, of both life and human nature, is counterbalanced by that of the deadly serious, the insipid, the wearisome – as is that of the light-hearted by the sombre, the gentle by the vicious, the refined by the vulgar, the wise by the stolidly fatuous. Many of us have been, either naturally or affectedly, any one of those things at different times, adjusting our attitude of mind to external influences and imperatives of circumstance. But no one has yet to see the world *as it is*. To do so would imply we can develop some understanding of *objective truth*. No chance; the world is not a monolith. The tension created by its diversity is the very thing that gives character to life. Were there no strain or contrast in human affairs, there would be no factionalism – no political parties, ideological stances, points of view, passionate dissent, tribal feuds or personal contretemps. That, it might be argued, would be a good thing. But utopia is not constituted of a world without internal points of conflict, without movement, progression or the dynamic of 'antithesis' as a challenge to the existing state of affairs. Such would surely make for a static, bleak, colourless existence, and a society that never grows, learns or develops by synthesising opposites, compromising, reconciling differences, resolving conflict. As biological organisms, humanity sprouted from the earth, from our planet's natural history and processes of evolutionary change and transformation. Little wonder that unstifled creativity and robust debate in all areas of activity are natural features of a free society. They are an extension of existence. In order to hold interest, a line of thought or point of argument is best accompanied by some 'counterpoint'. Processes of nature as well as significant disputations of public debate or of widespread renown among academic circles are best supplemented by a narrative of constructive engagement, illuminating them to fuller dimension and vibrancy. A directly confrontational alternative or antithetical polemic does not do this to any satisfactory extent. Hegel's conception of the 'antithesis' is not as that of a literal or diametrical opposite. It is, rather, a missing component of a pre-existing 'thesis' which completes the whole, producing a 'synthesis'. As a reaction (antithesis) to Papal excesses (thesis), the Reformation, far from *eradicating* Catholicism, *complemented* it, by introducing the second of two principal components which comprise modern Christianity (synthesis). A newly emergent whole is thus an enrichment of some incomplete original of itself which interacted with its own historic counterpoint. The world moves forward, not linearly; it hauls with it the full weight of every contrapuntal accretion to central ideas which propel it. But emotion and reason, as polar opposites, are manifestations of human sensibility and reflection, the full range of which is incalculable in variety, nuance and depth. They are features of human consciousness which demonstrate the *subjective* nature of how we perceive and function, showing that *all* experience is 'particular' and unique. And human consciousness is as varied as there are individual lives, with no common scope or purpose in support of meaning that's understandable to all.

Technology has transformed the severity of toil and labour in both hand and brain. It has eliminated virtually all aspects of work's former tribulations and made possible a level of creature comfort undreamt of in the past. But 'quality of life', 'well-being' and 'personal fulfilment', as linked to 'happiness', are intangibles which cannot be quantified or precisely measured, standing well outside the pursuit of material wealth or the convenience afforded by technical gadgetry. Is it possible we are unable to be fully, or even correctly, attentive to the simple business of 'living' owing to our preoccupation with the 'politics' *of* living? Have we not lost sight of something overwhelmingly significant through our obsessive engagement with daily distractions, false obligations and deluded priorities? Has not our focus dangerously shifted to the medium at the expense of the message? And must we not question the social consequences of the growing tendency for *uniformity of thought* as promoted by commercial interests, extending into nearly every area of life?

Nothing but time itself may be interminable, though some of us still write letters by hand, sing, wear shoes rather than trainers, and age gracefully. There can be no escape from the influence of our past or the intrusive currents of the present, nor can we remain unaffected by the problems of the world. We cannot evade the personal trials of living. But the secret of a fulfilled life may yet be sought in such as the practical wisdom to be extracted from Hotspur's remark in *Henry IV, Part 1,* "... out of this nettle, *danger,* we pluck this flower, *safety.*" We are all confronted with inescapable difficulties in 'life'. And we are locked in 'time'. There's no way out. Hotspur's example is not only wise to follow, *it is imperative.* It's *the best play*. There is little choice but to pluck the metaphorical flower, at every turn, in a barbed and intractable world. In fact, we've been doing so throughout the ages, by instinct. It should really come as no surprise. How else survival?

Welcome to the twenty-first century. Proceed with caution. And keep making *the best play*.

> *"If there be nothing new, but that which is*
> *Hath been before, how are our brains beguil'd,*
> *Which, labouring for invention, bear amiss*
> *The second burthen of a former child!"*
>
> – William Shakespeare